Knitting

Techniques and Projects

By the Editors of Sunset Books

Lane Publishing Co. • Menlo Park, California

An Ancient and Enduring Craft

Knitting is as old as the Egyptian pyramids—and as new as tomorrow's interstellar space vehicles. A folk craft once used to make silk stockings for American colonists, knitting today graces the sleek waists of top Parisian fashion models.

Why has this ancient craft endured throughout the centuries? Probably because knitting is so easy to learn. The knitting process consists of creating a series of interlocking loops of thread or yarn. Once you've mastered this technique, you've learned the basics of all knitting.

Knitting's simplicity is enhanced by its portability. A cloth bag or small basket is all you need to carry your work with you wherever you go. What's more, the low cost of knitting will enable you to create stylish garments at less cost than store-bought articles of similar materials and craftsmanship. To cut corners even more, see page 7 for ways to reuse yarn.

This *Sunset* knitting book is for all skill levels—and both sexes. Male-dominated knitting guilds in the 17th century developed standards and styles that took root. Today, men are once again realizing their potential as innovative knitters. For an example of male knitting know-how, see pages 24 and 25.

Whether you're a man or a woman, you'll find knitting a soothing craft. Work according to your own pace. If you're a beginner, zero in on projects rated for you. If you're an advanced knitter, you'll have fun elaborating on intermediate projects or discovering the unusual designs rated for highly skilled and experienced knitters. And if you're in between beginner and advanced, you'll find much to pique your enthusiasm and extend your skills.

Within the next 77 pages are all the techniques necessary to make any basic knitted garment and to complete any of the suggested projects. You can choose from among our collection of 35 original designs with step-by-step instructions.

Look especially at the sections called "Knit wit," which offer pearls of knitting wisdom gathered from professional knitters to make your efforts go more smoothly.

With the techniques you'll learn, and with a little inspiration, you can progress from your present level (even if you're a beginner) to designing your own creations and even inventing your own stitches. Projects and techniques work together to give the knitter a sound basis for exploring the world of knitting.

For their enduring patience and invaluable advice, we give special thanks to Jani Fellows, Barbara DiConza, Nancy Van Erden, Fiberworks, Gumps, Wild 'N Wooly, The Knittery, Pins & Needles, and Mon Tricot of Paris, France.

Edited by Robyn E. Shotwell

Design: Jerry Haworth

Artwork: Nancy Lawton

Photography: Jerry Wainwright. (Exceptions: Ted Mahieu, 46, 20–21, 61; Mon Tricot, 70.)

Front cover: Scenic sweater (pages 77-79) designed by Dione King, photographed by Ted Mahieu.

Back cover: (top) Scalloped scarf (page 45) designed by Jean Low, photographed by Jerry Wainwright; (bottom) Toasty mittens (page 61) designed by Rosalie Carl, photographed by Ted Mahieu.

Editor, Sunset Books: David E. Clark

Second Printing February 1978

Techniques

Projects

Contents

Project Rating Key

This symbol ▣▣ appearing throughout the Projects section is a guide to the skill level required to complete a project. Numbers indicate the following ratings:

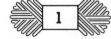 For beginners having only elementary skills

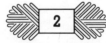 For intermediate-level knitters having basic skills

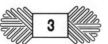 For experienced knitters who have mastered all conventional skills

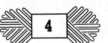 For advanced knitters who want a challenging project that requires special skills

An asterisk (*) appearing with a number indicates that the project becomes one skill level easier if it is knitted without the color pattern.

Techniques

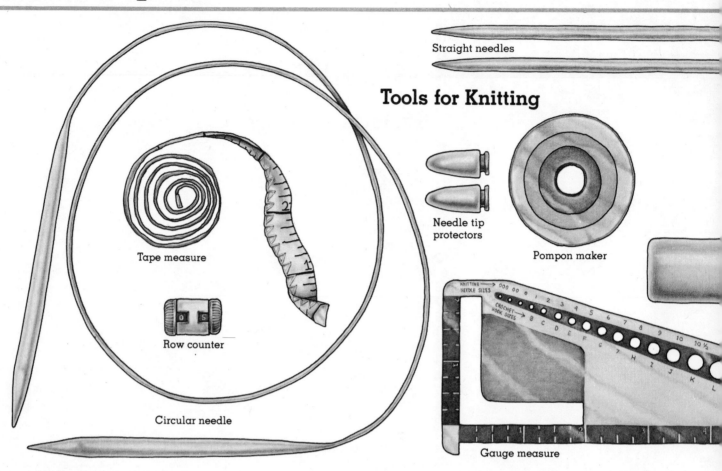

Straight needles

Tools for Knitting

Needle tip protectors

Pompon maker

Tape measure

Row counter

Circular needle

Gauge measure

This section introduces the basic techniques necessary to complete your first project.

All knitting begins with one motion — the looping of thread or yarn (or any spun, threadlike material) back and forth on two or more needles. This linking action creates an elastic fabric perfect for making sweaters, coats, caps, and countless other items.

How do you get started? All you need are two needles and a ball of yarn. The needles are your most important knitting tools.

Needle tips

When selecting your needles, look for ones that feel comfortable in your hands and that smoothly manipulate the yarn.

You can buy metal, plastic-coated metal, plastic, or wooden needles.

Most knitters use metal (aluminum) needles. They're easy to find and durable. Unfortunately, they tend to split yarn.

Plastic-coated metal needles are next in popularity because they combine the durability of metal with the smoothness of plastic — and they won't damage your yarn.

Plastic needles have been steadily losing popularity in recent years. They are difficult to find and tend to break easily. Some knitters prefer plastic needles, though, because they work so smoothly and quietly. If a needle breaks, you can insert the broken end into a pencil sharpener — the resulting short needle comes in handy for detailed knitting.

Wooden needles are the most difficult to find, but some knitters won't use anything else because they like the smoothness and natural feel of wood. Splinters

in the needle may sometimes cause yarn to snag; rub them with sandpaper or steel wool to keep them smooth.

Before buying a complete set of assorted size needles, experiment with several different types of needles to find the one you prefer. You'll save money if you buy all the needle sizes at once as a kit rather than one at a time.

Needles range from very thin (size 00) to very thick (size 17). In most cases the size needle you choose will depend on the weight of the yarn you're using — thick needles for bulky yarn, thin needles for fine yarn — and on the desired stitch gauge (see page 13 for gauge information).

Sometimes you'll find needles without any size indication. Use a gauge measure with needle holes

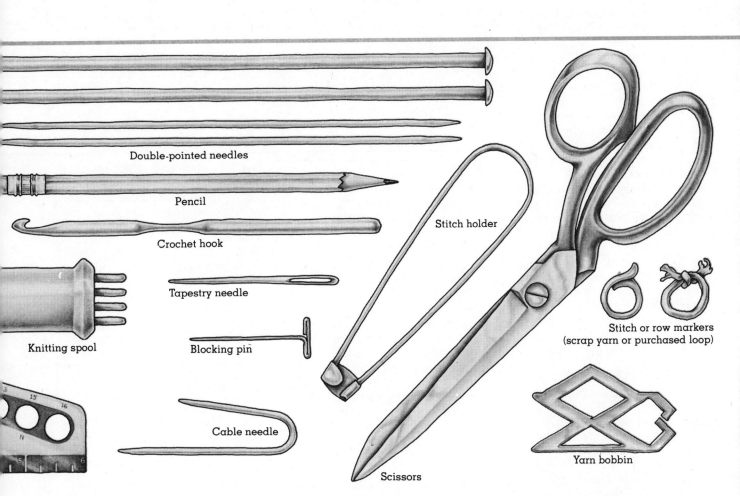

Double-pointed needles

Pencil

Crochet hook

Knitting spool

Tapestry needle

Blocking pin

Cable needle

Stitch holder

Scissors

Stitch or row markers
(scrap yarn or purchased loop)

Yarn bobbin

to determine the correct size of the needle. Simply slip the unmarked needle through the different holes until you locate a hole that barely clears the sides of the needle; note the needle size marked on that hole. (See drawing above of gauge measure with needle holes.)

Knit wit
- When choosing needles for a project, look for a color that contrasts with your yarn; this will make stitch counting easier.
- Sizes of European needles are marked in metric measurements. Consult a needle size conversion chart at a yarn shop to find equivalent American sizes. Since conversion charts are not always consistent, be sure to knit a test swatch to confirm the needle size conversion.

Needles come in two shapes— straight and circular. Straight needles are either single or double pointed. Single-pointed needles come in a set of two; double-pointed needles come in a set of four. Most knitting is done on straight needles. For practical tips on the use of circular needles, see page 13.

Caring for your needles is important if you want good results from your knitting. When stitches won't slide smoothly, wash your needles with soap and water, file any rough surfaces, and rub needles with paraffin.

Felt or cloth knife cases are useful for storing needles—just slip them into the individual pockets. You can also convert cardboard or plastic tubes into needle caddies. Seal one end of the tube with cardboard; store needles, points downward.

Avoid fastening plastic needles together with rubber bands. The rubber reacts with the plastic and causes the needles to deteriorate.

Fiber facts

Yarn is the best material for knitting. The range of yarn colors, textures, and weights is greater today than during any other time in knitting history.

High-quality yarn is elastic and durable, with lasting color and even texture.

All knitting yarn is either organic, synthetic, or a blend of organic and synthetic fibers.

The most resilient fibers are organic, such as those produced by sheep, alpacas, goats, and rabbits. These naturally elastic fibers stretch 30 percent when dry, 50 percent when wet—and still return to their original shape.

The most readily available and least expensive organic fiber is sheep's wool. The fiber structure and natural oils in wool make it the best insulator to keep you warm and dry long after other fibers become wet. People who live in icy climates rely heavily on wool clothing during the long, cold winters.

Other organic fibers (from alpacas, rabbits, worms, goats) are less available and more expensive than wool. They also require special care, but will appeal to knitters who desire unusual textures and unique yarn quality.

The alternative to organic fibers is chemically produced synthetic fibers. These contain some of the properties found in organic fibers but generally cost less.

Though they lack the warmth and resiliency of wool, synthetics such as orlon, dacron, polyester, acrylics, nylon, and rayon are often preferred for children's garments because they are easy to care for.

Some of today's most versatile yarn is a blend of organic and synthetic fibers, combining the best features of both. The fiber content of every yarn is marked on the package label, which also lists the percentage of each fiber in the yarn.

If you have some unidentified yarn, hold a small piece of it in a flame. If the yarn burns, it is organic; if it melts, it is synthetic.

Weight	Use	Gauge (see page 13)
Fingering (baby)	Lightweight garments, socks, dresses, blouses, baby garments	7–8 stitches = 1 inch on size 2 needles
Sport	Lightweight garments, afghans, socks, dresses	6 stitches = 1 inch on size 5 needles
Knitting worsted	Most garments, hats, gloves	5 stitches = 1 inch on size 9 needles
Bulky	Heavy jackets, sweaters	3 stitches = 1 inch on size 11 needles

Knit wit

- Be sure to maintain even tension when knitting with synthetics. Blocking (see page 19) won't compensate for irregularities caused by uneven tension.

Yarns come in various weights —from very thin yarn (fingering weight) to thick (bulky weight). The nature of your project will determine the correct yarn weight. For example, baby clothing requires a fine, lightweight yarn; winter jackets call for heavy, bulky yarn. The chart on this page describes the various weights of yarn, their uses, and their recommended stitch gauge (number of stitches per inch — see page 13).

If you find a yarn that you love, look for a project that requires this particular weight of yarn; then knit a swatch to determine if the stitch gauge matches the pattern requirements. You can make adjustments within the pattern to compensate for a slight discrepancy (see page 13).

Consider the washing instructions for a yarn before you buy it. For example, it is more practical to knit frequently washed children's garments with a machine washable synthetic than with an organic yarn that is difficult to care for.

Also consider the type of wear the garment will get. Handbags and children's toys, for instance, will last longer if made with durable rug yarn.

Before selecting a yarn, decide if your project will focus on the stitch pattern or on the yarn. A plain, solid-colored yarn can be enhanced by a decorative stitch pattern. You'll want to show off a fancy yarn (flaked, ombréd) to the best advantage, though, by eliminating any competition from an intricate stitch pattern.

Knit wit

- If you use a yarn with a slippery finish, add a strand of fingering yarn or cotton thread to help the garment maintain its shape.
- Yarn shops often provide free instruction with the purchase of yarn.

How much to buy

Yarn is sold by ounces or grams. The weight of an individual package of yarn is marked on the paper label. Patterns specify the amount of yarn to buy by referring to these weights.

Yardage is important, too. Make sure the yardage mentioned in a pattern corresponds to the yardage contained in each package of yarn. Yardages are indicated on special manufacturer's charts or on the yarn label.

If you use a stitch gauge other than the one required by your pattern, be sure to adjust the amount of yarn needed to complete the project.

It is always wise to buy extra yarn, or more than is called for in the pattern. You can usually return any unopened packages of yarn to the store where it was purchased.

Yarn winds up in a variety of shapes—pull-skeins, skeins, balls, hanks (same as skeins), and cones.

Skeins (loose, elongated coils) are the most common. Pull-skeins are close in popularity to skeins and are easier to use because you can pull the yarn from the center of the skein without tangles.

Some knitters prefer balls of yarn because they can work from the outside of a ball instead of the inside of a pull-skein. Skeins and hanks of yarn must be wound into balls—use a yarn swift or chair back, or ask a helpful friend to hold the yarn while you're winding.

Fine yarn, often used in machine knitting, comes on cones. Many knitters create their own color combinations by combining different plies of cone yarn to form a mixed strand of yarn.

Finding yarn is no problem. You can buy yarn at yarn shops, weaving supply stores, craft shops, department stores, dime stores, and directly from yarn factories.

If the homespun life style appeals to you, you can even buy sheep cuttings from mills in the United States and the British Isles and then spin and dye your own yarn.

A little about dye lots

Yarn is dyed in batches called lots. Color is consistent throughout a single lot, though it may vary as much as a complete shade between one dye lot and another.

When purchasing yarn for one project, make sure that all the yarn bears the same dye lot number. To be sure you don't run out, buy extra yarn for each project. Some shop owners will set aside extra skeins of the dye lot you've chosen until you finish your project. Be sure to retain yarn labels listing dye lot numbers for handy reference in case you need to buy additional yarn.

Knit wit

- If you must use yarn from different dye lots, knit alternating rows of each lot.

New old yarn

Remember that afghan you started last year and never finished? Don't despair—you can use that yarn on this year's project. First, unravel all the yarn and wind it loosely into a coil around your thumb and under your elbow; then use a contrasting color yarn to tie the old yarn into 2-ounce bundles or rings.

After the yarn is unraveled and wound into rings, it must be "dekinked." If you don't do this, the yarn will look kinky even after it is reknitted.

Use the following methods to dekink yarn:

For organics: Steam the yarn over a teakettle; or soak it in a cold water/vinegar solution and spin dry in a pillow case; or take the yarn to a dry cleaner for steaming.

For blends: Dampen yarn, wind it into a firm but not tight ball, and let dry overnight.

For synthetics: Use any of the methods suggested for organics or blends.

Knitter's shorthand

—A guide to abbreviations used throughout this book.

beg	beginning
ch	chain
dc	double crochet
dec	decrease
dp	double point
inc	increase
k	knit
p	purl
patt	pattern
psso	pass slipstitch over
rem	remaining
rnd	round
rep	repeat
sc	single crochet
sk	skip
sl	slip
st(s)	stitch(es)
tog	together
wyib	with yarn in back
wyif	with yarn in front
yo	yarn over
yon	yarn over needle
yrn	yarn around needle

The basics

One of knitting's great assets is its straightforward simplicity. Two stitches (knit and purl) plus casting on, increasing, and decreasing, are all the basic techniques needed to complete most elementary projects. Once you've mastered these techniques, you're on your way to knitting expertise.

Comfort first

Before picking up the needles, choose a comfortable place to sit. Make sure you have good light.

To find a relaxing way to hold your needles and yarn, try **A** and **B**; choose the position that suits you best. By keeping your hands on top of the needles and close to the points you can keep the stitches moving smoothly from one needle to another.

You'll find that most knitting instructions refer to the front and back of your needles. The side of the needles facing you is the front; the side away from you is the back. These terms relate only to the needles, not to your work.

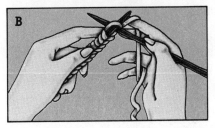

Casting on

The first step in knitting is to get the yarn onto the needles. This is done with a looping process called casting on. The loops made by casting on create the foundation for the first row of stitches.

Here are two popular techniques for casting on—one uses a single needle, the other uses two needles.

One-needle method: Measure out 1" of yarn for every st you want to put on your needle (30 sts is a good number to begin with). Make a slipknot at 30" mark; sl needle into knot. Two strands now hang from needle—one goes to ball of yarn; the other is 30" long.

Hold needle in right hand and yarn in left hand. Place short (30") strand over thumb. Yarn from ball goes over index finger. Both strands fall through center of palm (**A**).

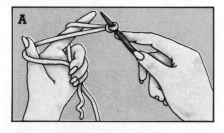

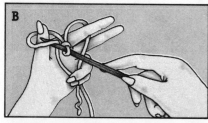

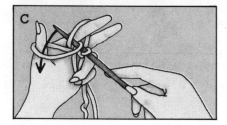

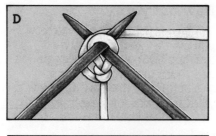

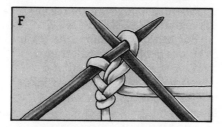

Insert needle from front to back under strand at left side of thumb (**B**). Throw yarn from index finger counterclockwise and pull through loop on thumb (**C**). Sl loop off fingers to needle.

If you are left-handed, adjust steps **A** through **C** since you will be holding your needle and yarn in reverse.

Two-needle method: Make slipknot 2" from end of yarn; sl left needle into knot. Insert right needle through loop from front to back. With right hand, place long strand over loop between needles, moving yarn counterclockwise (**D**). With right needle, guide strand down through loop, forming st on right needle. Sl st to left needle; gently pull long strand of yarn to tighten st (**E**).

To make next st, insert needle between new st and preceding st or slipknot (**F**); proceed as in steps **D** through **F**.

If you are left-handed, adjust steps **D** through **F** since you will be holding your needle and yarn in reverse.

Knit wit

- When learning casting on and other basic techniques, use size 8 or 9 needles and knitting worsted.
- Think "loose" when casting on. Most beginners are too tense, and stitches become so tight that they won't move along the needle.
- While casting on the first few stitches, you may want to hold the loops on the needle with your index finger.
- Use the one-needle method for a loose edge on casual, sporty garments, and the two-needle method for a firm edge on more formal garments.
- If you cast on too tightly, try using two needles as one. Slip one needle out when you're ready to begin knitting your first row.

Knit stitch

The knit stitch is a method of creating interlocking loops of yarn. This stitch appears smooth and has a chevron shape (**G**).

Hold needle with 30 cast-on loops in left hand. Hold other needle and yarn from skein in right hand. Insert right needle through first loop, front to back, forming an "X" with needles (**H**).

With right hand, pass yarn counterclockwise around right needle (**I**). Pull looped yarn through loop on left needle, forming a new st (**J**). Sl new st onto right needle; rep steps **H** through **J** with all rem loops.

Left-handed knitters hold yarn in left hand while working stitches from right to left.

Knit wit

- Knit through the front of the loop, never the back (unless increasing, see page 11).
- Don't split the yarn or pull through two strands of yarn at one time — you'll end up with more stitches than you started with.
- When you finish one row, turn your work around, keeping the empty needle in your right hand. Continue working stitches as before.

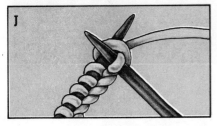

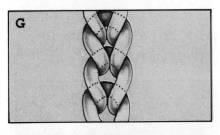

Purl stitch

The purl stitch also creates interlocking loops of yarn, but these loops have a nubby appearance (**K**). The procedure for the purl stitch is the reverse of that for the knit stitch. Practice the knit stitch first — then learning to purl will be much easier. The purl side of a knitted fabric is usually called the wrong side or the reverse side of your work.

Hold yarn in right hand as if doing knit stitch. Place needle with 30 cast-on loops in left hand and other needle in right hand. Insert right needle from back to front into front of the first loop on left needle. The yarn from the skein is in front of right needle. The needles form an "X."

With right hand, wrap yarn counterclockwise between two needles and around right needle (**L**). With right needle, pull yarn down and through loop on left needle (**M**). Sl new st onto right needle. Rep steps **L** and **M** for all rem loops.

After purling all loops, turn your work as in the knit stitch procedure. Continue purling.

Left-handed knitters hold yarn in left hand and work stitches from right to left.

Knit wit

- When working one knit stitch and one purl stitch alternately, be sure to change yarn from back to front (or vice versa) each time you switch from knit to purl (see ribbing, page 10).
- Knitters often purl more loosely than they knit. If you do this, hold yarn slightly tighter in your right hand on purl rows. Or, you can even out your row tension by using a smaller needle for the purl rows and the size the pattern specifies for the knit rows.

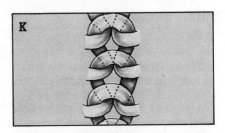

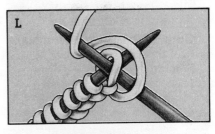

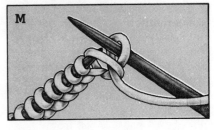

Stitch patterns

By combining knit and purl stitches, you can create textured patterns. Knitters have already discovered over 1,000 different stitch combinations, and today's devoted followers of the craft are still trying for more.

The following are some of the most popular stitch patterns:

Garter stitch—k all rows. Both sides of the fabric look alike (**A**).

Stockinette stitch—k 1 row, p 1 row. Rep these 2 rows (**B**). If you use the back side of this pattern as the right side of your work, the pattern is then called reverse stockinette stitch.

Seed stitch—Work an odd number of sts; k 1, * p 1, k 1, rep from * to end every row. Pattern looks the same on both sides of fabric (**C**).

Ribbing—Pattern varies depending on size of rib. For small rib: * k 1, p 1, rep from * to end. For larger rib, increase number of sts in each group of knit and purl sts. For example: k 3, p 3 (**D**).

Basket stitch—Work a number of sts divisible by 8. Rows 1, 2, 3, 4: * k 4, p 4, rep from * to end. Rows 5, 6, 7, 8: * p 4, k 4, rep from * to end. Rep these 8 rows (**E**).

Ridged lace stitch—Work a number of sts divisible by 6, plus 1. Row 1: * p 1, p 2 tog, yon, k 1, yrn, rep from * to last st, p 1. Row 2: p. Row 3: k. Row 4: p. Rep all 4 rows (**F**).

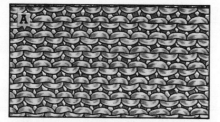

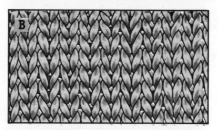

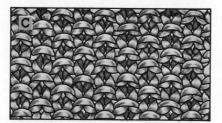

Cable stitch—Work on an even number of sts. Where cable occurs, sl half the cable sts to a cable needle (small double-pointed needle). Hold cable needle in back of work. Work other half of cable sts (**G**). Work sts from cable needle and finish row (**H**). Cable patterns vary in number of sts, size, shape, and yarn texture.

Popcorn stitch—Work on an even number of sts. Row 1: p. Row 2: * k 1, p 1, k 1 all into 1 st (increasing 3 sts in 1 st), p 3 tog (decreasing 3 sts in 1 st), rep from * to end. Row 3: p. Row 4: * p 3 tog, k 1, p 1, k 1 all into 1 st, rep from * to end. Rep rows 1 through 4 (**I**).

Increasing

Increasing the number of stitches on your needles will make knitted fabric wider.

Knitters use three techniques to increase: knitting a stitch twice, placing yarn over the needle, and knitting between stitches. All methods work on either the knit or purl side.

Knitting a stitch twice: k 1 without pulling st off needle. Place right needle to back of left needle. Insert needle into back loop of same st; k (**J**). Pull new st through loop and off needle (**K**). You now have 2 sts where you had 1.

Knit wit

- Knitting a stitch twice leaves a small bump on the right side of the fabric and is not desirable when using the stockinette stitch.

Yarn over method: On k side, bring yarn over needle to front of work as if to p. K next st, wrapping yarn as in normal procedure for knitting (**L**).

Knit wit

- The yarn over method creates holes where increases are located and is preferred for knitting lace stitch patterns.

Knitting between stitches: With right needle, pick up loop between sts (**M**). Place loop on left needle. K in back of loop (**N**).

Knit wit

- When lifting a loop between stitches, be sure to twist the stitch when placing it on the left needle. If you don't twist the stitch, a hole will result where you increased.
- Knitting between stitches is the most invisible of all the preceding methods for increasing.

Decreasing

Decreasing the number of stitches on your needles will make knitted fabric narrower.

There are two basic methods of decreasing: knitting two stitches together, and passing a slipstitch over a knit stitch. Decrease on the knit side whenever possible.

Knitting two stitches together: Insert right needle from front to back into 2 sts on left needle. K both sts tog; sl both loops off left needle to right needle (**O**).

Knit wit

- Knitting two stitches together causes the decrease stitches to slant to the right.
- If you purl two stitches together on the purl side, the decrease stitches will slant to the left.

Passing a slipstitch: With right needle, sl st to right needle without knitting. K 1. With left needle, pass slipped st to left over knitted st (**P**).

Knit wit

- Avoid twisting the stitch when slipping it to the right needle.

11

Knitting expertise

Knitters themselves are the best source of knitting know-how. By experimenting, making and correcting mistakes, and improvising, knitters acquire valuable experience in ways to make their work go smoothly. Here are some guidelines for gaining this expertise:

• If you leave your knitting on the needles for more than a few days, rip back a few rows before starting again. Needles stretch yarn, and blocking won't remove the looseness.

• When decreasing at both sides of a garment (for armholes, sleeve caps, or necklines), make your decrease only at the beginning of the rows. If you decrease at the beginning and end of rows, the beginning decrease is often tighter than the ending decrease. If decreasing is kept even, it will be easier to put seams together or to pick up stitches for ribbings.

• Bind off loosely (see page 15). If you bind off too tightly your garment will pucker and will not fit properly.

• Complete the entire row you're working before putting down your knitting. That way, stitches won't slip off your needle and you won't forget where you are in a pattern.

• If you drop a needle out of the first stitches of a row, try propping the right needle on your lap while wrapping the yarn, or hold both needles in one hand while wrapping the yarn with the other.

• Avoid laying the yarn on top of the needle — this results in an extra stitch or a hole in your work (see yarn over method of increasing, page 11).

• Maintain even tension throughout your work.

• Keep stitches moving smoothly and rhythmically over the needles.

• Splitting the yarn with a needle will cause puckers and extra loops on your needles. Always insert one needle *under* the other needle, not *through* the yarn.

• You can pick up dropped stitches several rows later with a crochet hook. On the *knit* side, loop the dropped stitch vertically, working from front to back (**A**). On the *purl* side work vertically, looping the dropped stitch through the back and over the next horizontal strand. Pull the horizontal strand through the loop on the crochet hook (**B**).

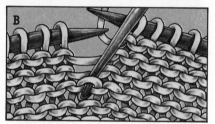

• If you've made a mistake many rows back, there's only one remedy — rip out all your work back to the mistake and correct it. The easiest part is taking the yarn off the needles and slowly unraveling each row, one by one. The trickiest part is getting the stitches back on the needle in the correct direction. Pick up the stitches from left to right, inserting the needle through the *back* of the stitch for the knit side (**C**), through the *front* of the stitch for the purl side (**D**).

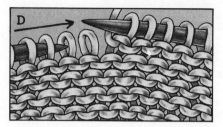

• *Always* check your stitch gauge before you begin. It never hurts to check it again if you stop working on the project for several weeks.

• Measure your work as you go. Check the measurements of a completed piece against the desired size.

• If you've dropped a stitch in the row you're working on, you can pick it up without ripping out any rows and without using a crochet hook. For a stitch dropped on the *knit* side, slip the dropped stitch onto the left needle with the long loose loop hanging to the back and right of the dropped stitch (**E**). With the right needle, slip the dropped stitch over the loose loop (**F**) and slide to the right needle (**G**). For a dropped stitch on the *purl* side, take your right needle and slip the dropped stitch to the left of the first stitch on the left needle (**H**). Insert your right needle from back to front through the center of the first stitch and on top of the loose loop (**I**). Use your right needle to push the loose loop down and through the center of the first stitch (**J**).

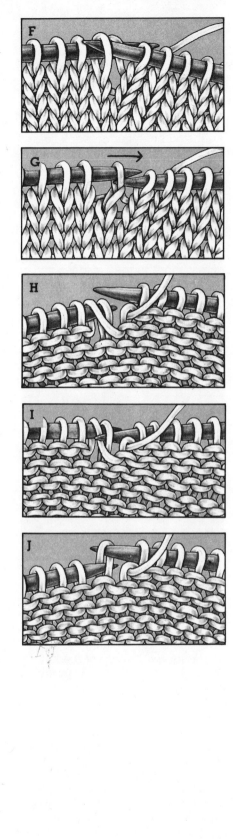

Adjust the stitch so that it faces the correct direction.

• When double-pointed needles are required for a project, begin by casting the total number of stitches onto one needle. Then divide the stitches evenly onto three double-pointed needles. All three needles are connected by yarn running from the last stitch on one needle to the first stitch on the next needle (see page 61). Work the stitches with the fourth needle in rounds. Avoid twisting stitches when moving from one needle to another.

• Use circular needles when working a large number of stitches (75 or more, using knitting worsted) or when you wish to eliminate seams. Work in rounds, not back and forth. To use circular needles as straight needles, turn your work at the end of each row. (See page 4 for a drawing of a circular needle.) If the project is heavy, circular needles will help to distribute the weight evenly.

The key — gauge

A knitting gauge indicates the number of rows and stitches to the inch. Matching your gauge with a pattern's required gauge is the most important step in knitting a project.

All knitting patterns are written to correspond to a specific gauge. If your tension doesn't give you the required gauge, your project won't turn out as indicated in the pattern.

Yarn weight and texture, needle size, and knitting technique all influence gauge. To determine your gauge, use the needle size indicated by the pattern for the main pieces. Check the gauge given in the pattern instructions (example: 5 sts=1 inch; 5 rows=1 inch).

Knit a swatch (test piece of knitted fabric) by casting on a multiple of that gauge. (If the gauge is 5 stitches to 1 inch, cast on 25.) Knit for 2 inches, working the stockinette stitch or the main stitch pattern used in the project.

Lay the swatch on a flat surface and measure across the entire width with a ruler, tape measure, or gauge measure (**K**). Find the gauge by dividing the number of stitches by the width (25 sts divided by 5 inches = 5 stitches to 1 inch). If your gauge equals the pattern's gauge, you're ready to begin the project.

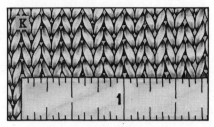

To get fewer stitches to the inch, change to larger needles or use a heavier weight yarn. Change to smaller needles or a lighter weight yarn to get more stitches to the inch. Keep working on the same swatch, measuring every 2 inches to compare the different gauges. Finally, use the needle size and yarn weight that give you the gauge indicated in the pattern.

To find the row gauge, count the rows vertically and use the same procedure that you used for finding stitch gauge.

Your tension (and gauge) may fluctuate while you knit, so measure as you go to ensure a consistent row and stitch gauge. Change needle size or adjust yarn tension as necessary to compensate for fluctuations in gauge. You can also adjust by increasing or decreasing the number of stitches per row (see page 11).

Knit wit
- Both front sides and sleeves of a cardigan will have the same gauge if knitted at the same time on one set of needles. Use a ball of yarn for each sleeve and side.
- It is easier to count rows of stockinette stitch on the purl side of your work, where rows appear as ridges.

Yarn joinery

When you finish a skein of yarn, tie or splice a new skein onto your work.

Tie on a new skein with a square knot, leaving 3 to 5 inches of yarn to weave into the fabric when the project is completed (see figure **C** under "Adding Color"). Always tie on the new skein at the beginning or end of a row, never in the middle.

You can splice on a new skein at any point in your work. First trim half the plies from the ends to be spliced. Thread the yarn end from the new skein with a tapestry needle. Weave the needle and yarn in and out of the remaining yarn end for 1 inch (**A**). Remove the needle and roll combined ends between your fingers.

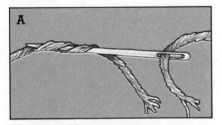

Stitch pick-up

Creating new stitches along necklines and borders is called picking up stitches. These stitches are loops pulled through the fabric. When picking up stitches, work from the right side of the fabric. The pattern will tell you how many stitches to pick up.

To evenly space the new stitches, divide the length of the edge into equal sections and pick up the same number of stitches in each section. Insert the needle or a crochet hook from the front to the back of your work through the edge stitch loops. Loop the yarn around the needle or hook and pull it through the fabric (**B**). Repeat this procedure for each new stitch.

Knit wit
- When picking up stitches on both edges of the front of a cardigan, remember to match the stitch spacing on both sides.
- If you change the length of any main pattern piece, remember to adjust the number of stitches to be picked up along the altered edges.

Adding color

Any project will acquire a dazzling personality if you knit it with multicolored yarns. You can add different colors of yarn to a pattern by knitting them in or by using the duplicate stitch.

Multicolor knitting

You can knit with different colors in two ways — tying on each color, or carrying over each color. For both methods (often called jacquard methods), graphs indicate which stitches are which colors. (See page 18 on graph reading.)

Tie on colors by breaking off the strand coming from the old color and tying on the new color with a square knot (**C**). Unfortunately, this method leaves a bulky knot wherever you change yarns.

If you carry each color behind your work the fabric gains a lush thickness without the bulging knots of the other method.

If you're working with a variety of small quantities of yarn, wrap a bobbin (a small, flat yarn

holder) with each separate color of yarn. Bobbins are simpler to work with than skeins because they're smaller and easier to manipulate. (See page 5 for a drawing of a bobbin.) For larger quantities of each yarn color, though, work directly from the skein.

Instead of tying on each color, simply bring up the strand with the next color you need from underneath your work and continue the row (**D**). Keep stitches loose and evenly spaced out.

Avoid carrying colors across more than 10 stitches. If your design requires you to carry across more than 10 stitches, twist the strands once so they won't snag on jewelry or fingers (**E**).

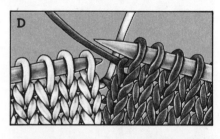

The duplicate stitch

This method of adding colors is employed after you've completed a project. Basically, you "duplicate" a knit stitch by embroidering on top of the knit stitch. For garments with many color changes, use of the duplicate stitch eliminates extra bulk and protruding knots.

You'll want to select the same weight yarn for your duplicate stitching as that used in the main fabric. Thread a tapestry needle with the new yarn and go in and out the same holes created by the original stitch. Work either from left to right, right to left, top to bottom, or bottom to top (**F**).

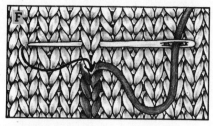

A graph will help you find the location and color of stitches to be embroidered.

Knit wit
- Keep the duplicate stitches loose to avoid puckering the fabric.
- Traditional embroidery techniques add color to knitting after a project is completed.
- Add color by using a crochet trim in a contrasting shade (see page 16).

Buttonholes

Knitted buttonholes blend with the handcrafted look of a knitted garment.

First, choose your buttons. The size of your garment and the desired number of buttons will determine the button size.

Buttonholes should begin ¼ to ½ inch from the garment's edge, depending on the garment itself and yarn weight used.

Eyelet buttonhole

(For garments made of fine yarn.) Work on the right side of fabric. Row 1: yo, k 2 tog. Row 2: k the yo. Rep rows 1 and 2 wherever you want a buttonhole (**G**).

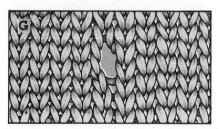

Vertical buttonhole

Use two balls of yarn. Divide work at desired buttonhole position. Work one side of buttonhole to button size using one ball of yarn. Use second ball of yarn to work other side to same position as first side. Work across both sides, joining yarn and continuing with original ball of yarn (**H**).

Horizontal buttonhole

Bind off number of sts required to accommodate button size at desired button location. On next row, turn work and cast on (directly over bound-off sts) the same number of sts as bound off. Turn work and continue to end of row. On the next row (3RD), work cast-on sts (**I**).

Knit wit
- With a tapestry needle and a single strand of yarn, use a simple overcast stitch to finish and reinforce the edges of the buttonhole.

Finishing

After all the time and loving care you've put into each row of your project, a well-done finishing job is essential.

Finishing really begins only after you've knitted all of the main pattern pieces. Finishing includes binding off, assembling the pieces, adding trim, blocking, and cleaning.

Binding off

When you've completed a pattern piece, you'll need to remove the stitches from the needles and give the knitted edge a neat appearance. This can be accomplished with the procedure called binding off.

With the sts on left needle, k 2 onto right needle. Insert left needle into front of first st on right needle. Lift this st over 2ND st and off right needle (**J**). You've just completed one bind off. K 1 onto right needle and rep procedure. Always bind off by beginning with 2 sts on right needle.

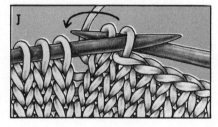

(Continued on next page)

Continue binding off all sts until 1 loop remains on right needle. Cut yarn 5" from loop. With right needle, pull loop of yarn until yarn end comes out of middle of last st (**A**).

Always bind off in a *loose* tension using the stitch you would use if you were proceeding with the pattern. That is, bind off in knitting on the knit side, in purling on the purl side, in ribbing, etc., as required by the pattern.

Skimming ends

After you've finished each pattern piece, work in all remaining loose yarn ends including the tail end left at the beginning of the cast-on row, any ends from yarn tied or spliced on during color changes, and the end left after binding off.

Thread each long end with a tapestry needle and weave through several plies of several stitches on the wrong side of the fabric until you run out of yarn. Tuck short ends under the stitches on the wrong side of the fabric with the point of the tapestry needle. Skim only the stitches that match the color of the yarn end.

Assembly

Once you've tucked in all loose yarn ends, you're ready to assemble the pattern pieces. Some knitters wash and block each pattern piece before assembly (see page 19).

Before assembling your project, identify each pattern piece—front, back, sleeve, and so on. Unless you plan to weave the seams, pin seams of pieces together with right sides facing.

Pin a sweater beginning with shoulder seams; next pin sleeve and then side seams.

You can sew, crochet, or weave seams together.

Sewing method: Use this method if your project is knitted with fine or medium-weight yarn.

Thread a tapestry needle with the same color yarn used in your project. Using a simple backstitch, sew seams together, keeping the yarn tension even and loose. As you sew, match pattern rows, colors, and pattern pieces. Sew ⅛ inch in from the fabric edge (**B**).

Crochet method: Crocheted seams look smooth and professional. Crochet the seams of projects knitted with fine or medium-weight yarn.

Use a crochet hook of the appropriate size for the yarn weight in your project. (Consult a yarn shop for a hook size chart.) Generally, small hooks work with lightweight yarn; large hooks with bulky yarn. Use matching yarn and slipstitch the seams together through the two top edge stitches, keeping tension even (**C**).

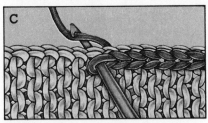

Weaving method: Weave seams to join knitted fabrics horizontally. With bulky yarns you must use this method (also called grafting or kitchener stitch) to achieve smooth, invisible seams.

Thread a tapestry needle with matching yarn. Each piece to be seamed should have the same number of rows or stitches.

Hold the fabric edges together with right sides facing you. Insert the needle through the first stitch on the bottom left edge, from the bottom to the top of the fabric. Place the needle through the next stitch on the right-hand side, from bottom to top. Alternate this staggered pattern, keeping tension even while matching rows and stitches (**D**).

Knit wit

- Block or steam-press all finished seams.

Crocheted finishes

A knowledge of crochet is a useful addition to a knitter's repertoire.

Use the *chain stitch* to make ties, fasteners, and belt loops. Attach yarn to crochet hook using a slipknot (**E**). With hook in right hand and yarn in left hand, wrap yarn over hook and pull through loop on needle (**F**). Work a chain the desired length by repeating this looping process.

Single crochet trims give a refined edge to a knitted project. Insert hook through two loops of the edge stitches. Wrap yarn around hook and pull through top two edge loops to get one loop on hook (**G**). Insert hook through next two top loops on fabric edge and wrap yarn around hook; pull yarn through loops to get two loops on hook (**H**). Wrap yarn around hook and pull through the two loops on your hook, leaving one loop on hook (**I**). Continue working steps **H** and **I** until trim is completed.

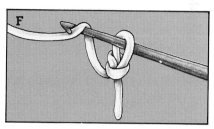

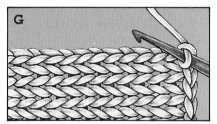

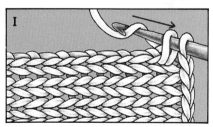

Knit wit

- Before crocheting a trim, divide each edge into halves, quarters, and (if long) eighths; mark with pins. Crochet an equal number of stitches between pins for even placement of stitches.
- If you're trimming a sweater, begin crocheting at the bottom edge of the right front side seam.

Fringe and tassels

Add fringe or tassels to your work to soften the appearance of the project, to complement the color scheme, or to give the edges of the project a more finished look.

To make fringe, cut a piece of cardboard 6" long and twice as wide as the desired length of fringe (4" wide if you want fringe 2" long). Wrap yarn around width of cardboard; cut strands at top and bottom of cardboard (**J**). Determine how many strands thick you want your fringe. Fold *half* of that number in half. Use a crochet hook to pull a group of strands through fabric edge from back side to front side (**K**). Pull cut ends through loop and tighten (**L**).

To make a tassel, cut a piece of cardboard 6" long and as wide as the desired length of the tassel. Wrap yarn around width of cardboard. Tie a piece of yarn around the strands at the top (**M**). With scissors, cut strands at the bottom. Tie another piece of yarn ⅓ the distance down from the top of the tassel, wrapping yarn around strands several times; fasten end (see page 32, figure A). Trim all ends. Attach tassel to finished project with yarn and a tapestry needle. Make desired number of tassels and space evenly around borders.

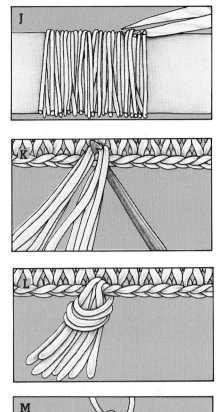

Sizing up

Before purchasing yarn for a project, read your pattern carefully to determine the size that corresponds to your body measurements. Different sizes often require different amounts of yarn.

Patterns either mention the finished size of the garment or list body measurements that relate to size classifications. Sizes marked small, medium, large, or 8, 10, 12 vary for each pattern company. Refer to body measurements to ensure that the pattern company's size 8 is also *your* size 8. In this book, all patterns relate to body measurements.

Some garments are designed to fit close to the body; others are loose-fitting. Adjust the size to match the way you prefer clothing to fit.

(Continued on next page)

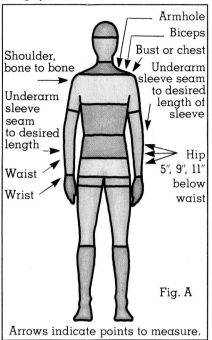

Arrows indicate points to measure.

Labels on Fig. A:
- Armhole
- Biceps
- Bust or chest
- Shoulder, bone to bone
- Underarm sleeve seam to desired length of sleeve
- Underarm sleeve seam to desired length
- Waist
- Wrist
- Hip 5", 9", 11" below waist

Fig. A

To determine your size, take an accurate set of your body measurements. Have someone measure you with a tape measure, making sure to place one finger between your body and the tape for all width measurements.

Take children's measurements with growth in mind. Make a child's garment a little large; cuff the sleeves until the child grows into the garment.

If you must guess at someone else's size, be conservative. You can make a garment one or two sizes larger by blocking (depending on the yarn), but you can't make it smaller.

The lines on figure A indicate where to measure your body. Make a list of these measurements to have on hand for future projects.

Pattern adjustments require increasing or decreasing the number of stitches or rows in the pattern. Your stitch and row gauge tells you how many stitches or rows to add or subtract per inch of adjustment (see page 13).

Knit wit
- Bust measurements are *not* bra size.

Grasping graphs

Graphs or charts provide a visual map of pattern colors and eliminate laborious reading of instructions for color changes.

A graph of squares portrays the fabric area that contains the colored design. Each square represents a stitch; each horizontal line of squares equals one row of stitches. Usually you read a chart from bottom to top.

The method of reading a chart depends on whether you're knitting in rows or in rounds. With rows, the first row (usually the right side of the fabric) is read from right to left. The next row (usually a purl row) is read from left to right (B). If working in rounds, read from right to left for *every* row. Each round is the right side of the fabric.

Some charts are marked for different sizes and indicate repeats across rows. If the chart isn't printed in color, symbols are used to represent different colors (for example, a triangle may equal red, a circle blue).

When knitting a charted garment, match your row and stitch gauge to the gauge specified in the pattern instructions. For instance, if you work more stitches to the inch than the pattern gauge specifies, your design will come out too small.

For techniques for changing colors as indicated on a graph, see pages 14 and 15.

Fig. B

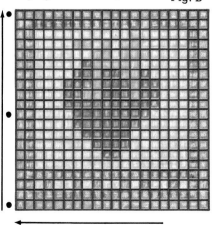

Arrows indicate direction for reading chart.
Dots are placed at 10-row intervals.

Pattern reading

Some knitting patterns explain every step and finishing detail; others give only general guidelines. All patterns, though, break down into the following sections:

- Description of the project
- Materials needed
- Sizes; body measurements
- Gauge
- Step by step instructions for shaping pattern pieces; stitch patterns; graphs
- Finishing details

Before beginning a project, read completely through the pattern instructions. Look for new techniques and sections that require special attention or practice. Circle the quantities of materials and the numbers of stitches and rows that relate to your size — if a pattern is written for more than one size, stitch counts and material quantities for other sizes are given in parentheses.

Verify the pattern sizing before casting on your first stitches. Begin by locating the number of stitches for your size from armhole to armhole (before shaping begins). Divide that number by the number of stitches per inch indicated in the stitch gauge. This will give you the number of inches of fabric on your needle for half the bust or chest measurement. Double this figure — the sum should correspond to your chest or bust measurement. If it doesn't, consider adjusting the gauge by using larger or smaller needles, or knit the garment in the next size.

Check the materials list. Buy enough yarn of one dye lot (see page 7) to complete the pattern in your size. Buy the specified yarn weight.

If you want to substitute yarn, you'll need to compare yardages. Your yarn dealer probably has yarn substitution charts that give specific yardage information for various brands.

Check the per-skein yardage for the yarn specified; then multiply that figure by the number of skeins called for and you'll know the total yardage you need.

Next, refer to the chart to find the per-skein yardage for the yarn you want to substitute; divide that figure into the total yardage you need to complete the pattern and you'll know how many skeins to buy.

The materials list indicates the needle size or sizes to give you the required gauge with the specified yarn. Gauge is always mentioned in an accurate pattern. Check your gauge to see if you should change the needle size (see page 13).

The materials list also includes notions such as buttons, stitch holders, and row counters.

Practice new or complicated stitch patterns before you begin. You will be aware of any problems or change of gauge at this point.

Most patterns use abbreviated knitting terms; refer to page 7 for a key to all abbreviations used in this book.

A pattern may tell you to knit to "desired length"; if so, replace the pattern length measurements with *your* preferred length measurements.

Measure your work as you go. Mark your place in pattern instructions and keep track of the number of rows for stitch patterns. Make any notations of alterations so that the next time you follow the same pattern you'll have the necessary changes at your fingertips.

Washing wisdom

Take each completed piece of knitted fabric and place it in a tub of cold water. Add a gentle soap (not detergent) and allow the piece to soak 3 minutes, agitating gently once or twice. Carefully squeeze out the soapy water.

Rinse each piece well with cold water and *gently* squeeze out the excess moisture. Some knitters put the wet pieces into a closed nylon bag or pillow case and then in a washer; set the washer on the spin cycle, and whirl out excess moisture. Do not stretch, pull, or hang the piece. Yarn—especially synthetic yarn—will stretch out of shape when wet.

After the moisture is removed, gently lay out each piece on a turkish towel. Allow the pieces to dry away from direct sunlight.

Knit wit
- Wash acrylic yarns in a machine and use the dryer as you would for other synthetic fabrics.
- If you prefer, you can assemble your project first and then wash it. Follow the same procedure used for washing unassembled pieces.

Blocking

Cold water or hot steam provides knitted garments or other knitted projects with the desired shape. This process—called blocking—gives a project a finished, professional quality.

Some knitters like to block a garment before it is assembled; others block assembled garments. If you block the pieces separately, you can adjust each one to equal the desired measurement for each piece. If you block an assembled garment, you can match seams and stitch patterns, and adjust the size.

Block a project while it is moist, either just after washing or when it has been rewet with a spray mister. (Roll the pieces in a turkish towel to keep them moist.)

Blocking is best done on a large, flat surface out of direct sunlight where the garment can be left to dry completely. Place a bedpad or large towel on a large piece of plywood or particle board. Arrange the garment or one garment piece right side up

on the board. Adjust size and even out borders. Avoid stretching the fabric too much—it will lose its fluffy appearance. With your fingers and the palms of your hands, press down on the fabric to make it lie smooth and flat. Some knitters prefer to use pins along the edges to hold the fabric in place; pins may leave marks on blocked garments, though.

Lightly steam-press the main pieces on the right and wrong sides. Press the seams if the garment is already assembled. Leave garment in place and allow to dry completely.

Knit wit
- Knitted size is different from blocked size. For example, if a chest measurement is 36 inches, the blocked size of unassembled front and back pieces is 38 inches (seam allowance requires extra fabric).
- If you're blocking a cardigan, start with the back. Then block both fronts on top of each other and both sleeves on top of each other to ensure identical size and shape.
- Some knitters make a paper pattern of the desired size of each piece, place the pattern under the garment, and block or adjust the fabric to fit the pattern.

Knit care

All knits will keep their shape best if folded and stored in a drawer. Never hang a knitted garment on a clothes rack, hanger, or hook—it will grow two to three sizes larger, depending on the type of yarn. Avoid placing garments in plastic bags or boxes where moisture will collect and deteriorate the fibers.

Projects

This section offers a collection of original designs for beginning to advanced knitters. To help you select a project, we've rated each one according to skill level (see page 3).

Included in these 34 tantalizing designs are traditional-style sweaters, avant-garde clothing, knitted objects to enhance your home, and innovative accessories to accent your wardrobe.

Before starting any project, carefully read the preceding techniques section for important information about materials, stitches, gauge, sizing, and finishing.

Afghan of bands

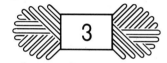

For explanation of project rating, see pg. 3.

Eleven long, knitted panels are woven together to make this cozy afghan. The design is by Helen Kisch.

You'll need: Knitting worsted — 16 ounces *each* of plum (P) and lavender (L), 12 ounces of raspberry (R); size 8 straight needles; F or G crochet hook; tapestry needle.

GAUGE: 5 stitches=1 inch
6 rows=1 inch

SIZE: 50 by 68"

Step by step

For key to abbreviations, see pg. 7.

PANELS—(Make 11: 4 *each* P and L, and 3 R.) Cast on 29 sts; k 2 rows. Beg patt st.

Stitch patt: Row 1: k 2, inc 1, k 5, p 6, p 3 tog, p 6, k 5, inc 1, k 2. **Row 2** (and all even-

numbered rows through row 14): k 2, p 25, k 2. **Row 3:** k 2, inc 1, k 6, p 5, p 3 tog, p 5, k 6, inc 1, k 2. **Row 5:** k 2, inc 1, k 7, p 4, p 3 tog, p 4, k 7, inc 1, k 2. **Row 7:** k 2, inc 1, k 8, p 3, p 3 tog, p 3, k 8, inc 1, k 2. **Row 9:** k 2, inc 1, k 9, p 2, p 3 tog, p 2, k 9, inc 1, k 2. **Row 11:** k 2, inc 1, k 10, p 1, p 3 tog, p 1, k 10, inc 1, k 2. **Row 13:** k 2, inc 1, k 11, p 3 tog, k 11, inc 1, k 2.

These 14 rows form 1 complete patt. Work a total of 18 patts. Then work final patt, decreasing for scallop as follows: **Row 1:** (right side) k 6, p 2 tog, p 5, p 3 tog, p 5, p 2 tog, k 6. **Row 2** (and all even rows): k 1ST and last 2 sts. p center sts. **Row 3:** k 5, p 2 tog, p 4, p 3 tog, p 4, p 2 tog, k 5. **Row 5:** k 4, p 2 tog,

p 3, p 3 tog, p 3, p 2 tog, k 4. **Row 7:** k 3, p 2 tog, p 2, p 3 tog, p 2, p 2 tog, k 3. **Row 9:** k 2, p 2 tog, p 1, p 3 tog, p 1, p 2 tog, k 2. **Row 11:** k 2, p 2 tog, p 1, p 2 tog, k 2. **Row 13:** k 2, p 3 tog, k 2. **Row 14:** Bind off rem sts, leaving 12' tail.

FINISHING —Join panels tog following this order: P, L, R, P, L, R, L, P, R, L, P. With right sides facing, beg at scallop edge with 12' end. Work 1 row sc around scallop, working 3 sc in center, ch 1; do not turn. Work 1 row reverse sc (see pg. 49). Pull up loop of next 12' end through loop on hook and work next scallop. Rep this procedure to end of afghan. Attach 12' tails and work other side the same way; work in ends.

Lacy afghan

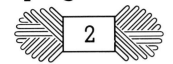

2

For explanation of project rating, see pg. 3.

Chilly winter evenings will feel less blustery when you're wrapped up in this lacy afghan. The design is by Mary Walker Phillips.

You'll need: Knitting worsted — 12 ounces ginger (G), 8 ounces purple (P), 20 ounces brick (B); size nine 29" circular needle; tapestry needle; stitch markers; cardboard; scissors.

GAUGE: 4 stitches = 1 inch
11 rows = 2 inches

SIZE: 49 by 68"

Knit wit
- Rows are worked back and forth, not in rounds.

Step by step

For key to abbreviations, see pg. 7.

MAIN BODY—Cast on 194 sts with B, placing markers on needle after first 4 sts and before last 4 sts. (These sts are not worked in patt. They are always worked in garter stitch —see pg. 10—for hem.)

Begin hem: Work 5 rows in stockinette stitch (see pg. 10); k 1 row; work stockinette stitch for 6 rows; k 1 row.

Stitch patt: (multiple of 8 sts plus 2) Patt worked on sts between markers *only.* **Row 1:** k 1, *k 2, k 2 tog, yo, k 4, rep from * to end, k 1. **Row 2:** p across.
Row 3: k 1, *k 1, k 2 tog, yo, k 1, yo, sl 1, k 1, psso, k 2, rep from * to end, k 1. **Row 4:** k 1, *k 2, p 5, k 1, rep from * to end, k 1.
Row 5: p 1, *p 1, k 5, p 2, rep from * to end, p 1. **Row 6:** Same as row 4. **Row 7:** k 1, *k 6, k 2 tog, yo, rep from * to end, k 1. **Row 8:** Same as row 2.
Row 9: k 1, *yo, sl 1, k 1, psso, k 3, k 2 tog, yo, k 1, rep from * to end, k 1. **Row 10:** p 1, *p 3, k 3, p 2, rep from * to end, p 1.
Row 11: k 1, *k 2, p 3, k 3, rep from * to end, k 1. **Row 12:** Same as row 10.

These 12 rows complete patt. Afghan is made by rep complete patt as follows: 3 times in B, 3 in G, 2 in B, 3 in P, 2 in B, 3 in G, 2 in B, 3 in P, 2 in B, 3 in G, 3 in B.

Hem: p 2 rows. Work 5 rows stockinette, k 1 row, work 6 rows stockinette. Bind off in last p row.

FINISHING—Fold hem after blocking; sew across row. Rep at both ends.

Tassels: Make 60 tassels (20 of each color) 6" long, 8 strands thick (see pg. 17). Attach tassels on right and left sides where there is a color change. Attach 3 tassels —1 *each* G, P, B —at every color change, using odd or 3RD color in middle. When all tassels are attached, trim.

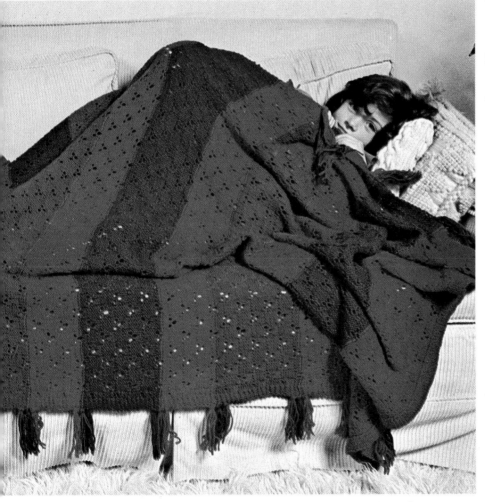

Poetic vest

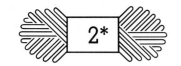

2*

For explanation of project rating, see pg. 3.

If you're an aspiring poet (or even if you've never made a rhyme), try this loose-fitting jacket that whispers its message to every beholder. The designer wrote the lilting phrase, "birds fly over the rainbow," using the duplicate stitch. A crocheted tie fastens the jacket at the neck. The design is by Linda Mendelson.

You'll need: Fingering yarn — 10½ ounces cream (C), 3½ ounces *each* of red (R), orange (O), yellow (Y), blue (B), green (G), and magenta (M); size 6 straight needles; size six 29″ circular needle; size F crochet hook; tapestry needle; stitch holder; stitch markers.

GAUGE: 19 stitches=4 inches
6 rows=1 inch (using 3 strands)

SIZE: Bust=36″ (38″, 40″)
Instructions are for size 36; changes for other sizes are in parentheses.

Knit wit
- The right side of the sweater is purl side on the yoke, knit side on the bottom.
- Use 3 strands as listed. (Example: RRR=3 strands of red.)

Step by step
For key to abbreviations, see pg. 7.

YOKE —Starting at bottom of back and using triple strands of R and size 6 straight needles, cast on 100 (110, 120) sts. **Row 1:** k. **Row 2:** (right side) k 6, p to last 6 sts, k 6. Repeating last 2 rows and following color patt (see fig. A) work 42 rows. **Row 43:** k across 33 (38, 43) sts, sl

Color Pattern
Fig. A

Work 4 rows each:
RRR, RRO, ROO, OOO, OOY, OYY, YYY, YYG, YGG, GGG, GGB, GBB, BBB, BBM, BMM.

Work 18 rows:
MMM.

Work 4 rows each:
BMM, BBM, BBB, BBG, BGG, GGG, GGY, GYY, YYY, YYO, YOO, OOO, OOR, ORR, RRR.

marker on needle, k 34, sl marker on needle, finish row. **Row 44:** k 6, p 27 (32, 37), k 34, p 27 (32, 37), k 6. **Row 45:** k. Rep last 2 rows until you finish row 50. **Row 51:** k 39 (44, 49) sts; sl to holder. Bind off center 22 sts, k rem 39 (44, 49) sts.

Continue working in stitch and color patt until 96 rows are completed (GGB). **Row 97:** Using GGG, cast on 11 sts at center edge. Work 7 rows, knitting 17 sts at center edge every row; return to stitch patt and work until 4TH row of RRR is completed; bind off.

(Continued on page 24)

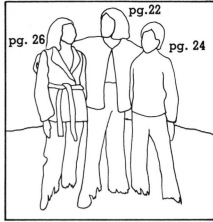

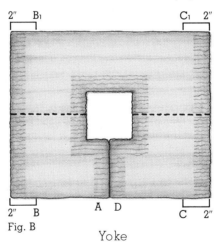

Fig. B   Yoke

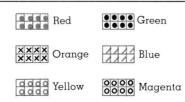

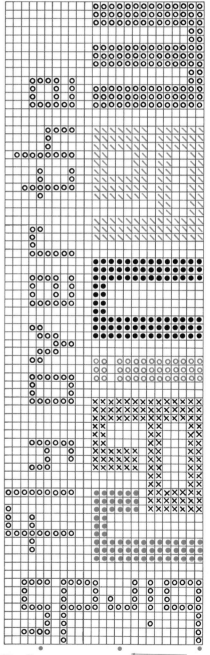

Fig. C

Dots are placed at 10-row intervals.

Arrows indicate direction for reading chart.

Jacquard pattern on back

Phrase worked in duplicate stitch

Navajo motif on front

Sl sts from holder to needle, join yarn to first st and work same as 1ST half.

BODY—Measure 2" for each corner (see fig. B). Fold piece so B and B₁, and C and C₁ meet. Make sure p side is outside. Using circular needle and CCC, starting at point A, pick up and k 42 (45, 47) sts between A and B, 85 (90, 95) sts between B (B₁), C (C₁), and 42 (45, 47) sts between (C₁) and D (170, 180, 190) sts. Place stitch markers where front and back join. **Row 1:** (wrong side) k 6, p to last 6 sts, k 6. **Row 2:** k. Rep these 2 rows for 14 (15, 16)", increasing 1 st at each marker every 12 rows. K all sts for 8 rows; bind off loosely.

CROCHET TRIM—Join CCC at bottom right front edge. Work 1 row sc up right front, around neckline, and down left front, working 3 sc in corner sts; fasten off. Using CCC, join underarm seams and work 1 row sc around sleeve edges.

TIES—(Make 2.) Using CCC, ch 50. Work 1 sc in 2ND ch from hook and in each ch to end. Sew 1 tie to each side of neck.

EMBROIDERY—Using a triple strand of yarn and tapestry needle, embroider design in duplicate st (see pg.14–15) following fig. C, pg. 22.

Navajo sweater

See color photo, page 23.

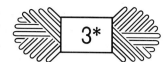

3*

For explanation of project rating, see pg. 3.

Many of today's designers incorporate ethnic themes in their clothing designs. For example, this turtleneck sweater with raglan sleeves has Navajo rug motifs on the front and is solid red on the back. The colors are those most often used in traditional Navajo rugs — reds, white, black, and brown. The design is by Charles Harrison.

You'll need: Knitting worsted — 12 (12, 16) ounces *each* of red and maroon (R), 4 ounces *each* of black and chocolate brown (B), 2 ounces white (W); sizes 8 and 10 straight needles; size eight 16" circular needle; 4 stitch holders; stitch markers.

Knit wit

- Sweater knitted using 2 strands of yarn, except last few rounds of neck. White (W)=2 strands white; black (B)=1 strand black, 1 strand brown; red (R)=1 strand red, 1 strand maroon.
- You will have fewer knots to untangle when working pattern areas if you first wind the wool using 2 strands. (Example: Wind 1 ball with the 2 reds together.)
- Variegated effect in pattern area is achieved by carrying color not used, looping it around working strand after every other stitch.
- Alternate loops of carried color after even-numbered stitches on one row and after odd-numbered stitches on next row.
- Carry strands *loosely.*

GAUGE: 4 stitches=1 inch
5 rows = 1 inch
(stockinette stitch on size 10 needles)

SIZES: Bust=32" (34", 36") Instructions are for size 32; changes for other sizes are in parentheses. Sweater is planned for 16" from beginning to underarm. If you wish to lengthen sweater, add half of the additional length before beginning chart.

Step by step

For key to abbreviations, see pg. 7.

FRONT—Using size 8 straight needles and R, cast on 68 (72, 76) sts. Work in k 1, p 1 ribbing for 2". Change to size 10 straight needles and work in stockinette stitch (see pg. 10) for 2", ending with purled row.

Next row: k 8 (10, 12) sl marker on needle, join B to next st and k across 52 sts of 1ST row of fig. A; sl marker on needle. With R, k 8 (10, 12). As you continue in patt, do not carry W strands beyond last B or W sts in any row except row before each crossbar. Carry the strand behind 6 extra sts so it will be positioned for the first st in next row. Continue in stockinette stitch, working sts between markers in patt until front measures 16" or desired length to underarm, ending with purled row.

Shape raglan: Dec 1 st each side every k row until 32 (34, 36) sts rem, ending with purled row.

Shape neck: k 2 tog, k until 6 sts rem on right needle. Sl center 18 (20, 22) sts to holder. Attach 2ND ball R to next st and finish row. Dec 1 st each neck edge every k row, while decreasing at side edges as before. No sts rem.

BACK —Work same as front, omitting patt, until back measures same as front to underarm, ending with purled row.

Shape raglan: Dec 1 st each side of back every k row until 24 (26, 28) sts rem; sl to holder.

SLEEVES — (Make 2.) Using size 8 straight needles and R, cast on 34 sts. Work in k 1, p 1 ribbing for 2", increasing 1 st at end of last row. Change to size 10 straight needles. Beg with p row, work in stockinette stitch for 3 rows. Fasten off R. Join B and beg fig. B, working through 12 rows of patt. Fasten off B and W. Join R and inc 1 st each side, then every 2 (1½, 1½)" five (7, 9) times more. Work even on 47 (51, 55) sts until sleeve measures 16 (17, 18)" or desired length to underarm.

Shape raglan: Dec 1 st each side of sleeve every k row until 6 (8, 10) sts rem; sl to holder.

Arrows indicate direction for reading chart. Dots are placed at 10-row intervals.

Fig. B

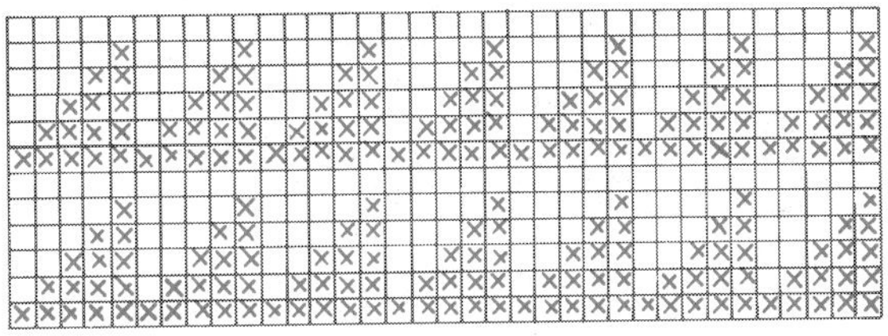

Chocolate brown
Black
White
Maroon
Red

Fig. A

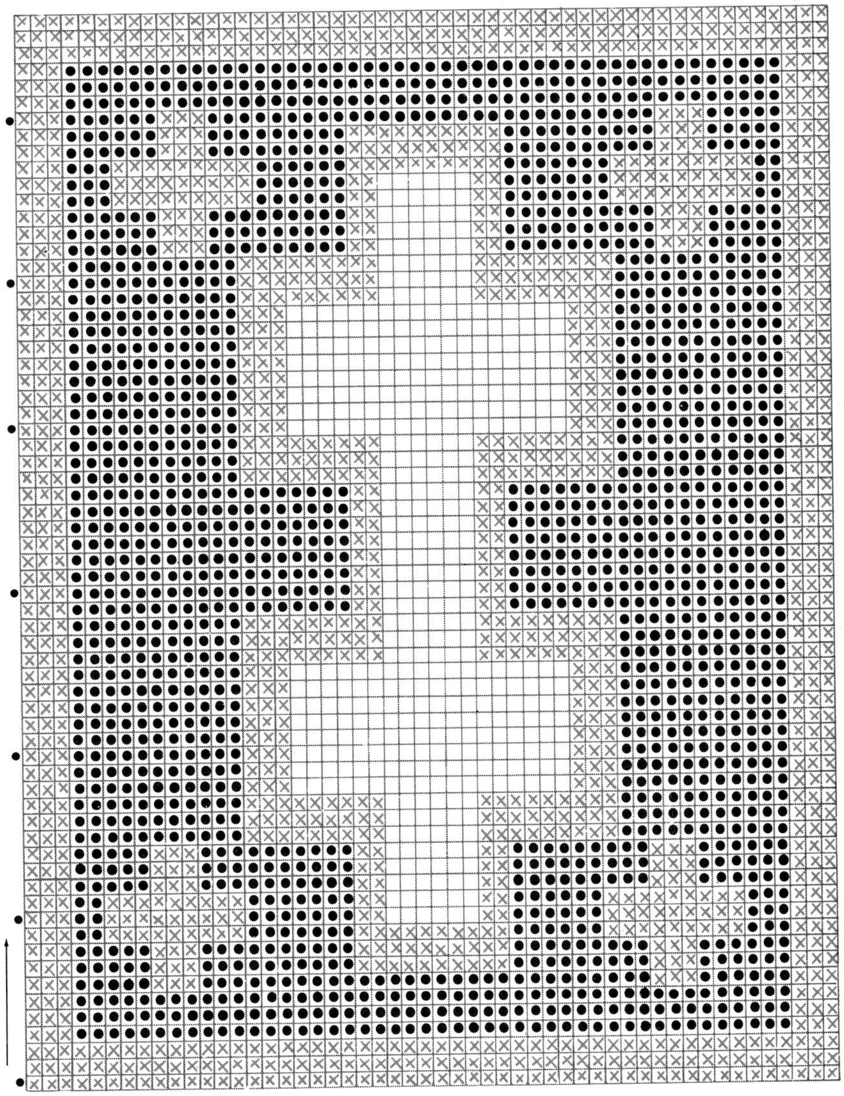

FINISHING —Join raglan, side, and sleeve seams.

Neck: Join R to first st on back neck stitch holder. Using circular needle, k off 24 (26, 28) sts from holder, *6 (8, 10) sts from top of sleeve*. **Pick up and k 6 sts along shaped neck edge**, k off 18 (20, 22) sts from front stitch holder. Rep from ** to ** once and * to * once. Put marker on needle. Work in k 1, p 1 ribbing on 66 (74, 82) sts for 2". Fasten off maroon strand. Using rem red strand, continue in ribbing for 3½" more. Bind off loosely in ribbing.

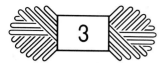

Sweater jacket

See color photo, page 23.

3

For explanation of project rating, see pg. 3.

Brilliantly colored pyramids embellish the sleeve caps, yoke, and lapels of this sweater jacket. The jacket is belted around the center ribbed section and has flared sleeves and two pockets. The design is by Diane Katz and Martha Ehlers.

You'll need: Knitting worsted — 28 ounces tan (T), 8 ounces rust (R), 2 ounces *each* of yellow (Y), green (G), red (RD), white (W), and orange (O); sizes 5 and 9 straight needles; size nine 29" circular needle; stitch holder; tapestry needle; size 2 steel crochet hook.

GAUGE: 9 stitches=2 inches 6 rows=1 inch (in stockinette stitch on size 9 needles)

SIZE: Bust=33" (35", 36") Instructions are for size 33; changes for other sizes are in parentheses.

Step by step

For key to abbreviations, see pg. 7.

BACK — Using size 9 straight needles and R, cast on 86 (90, 94) sts. **Row 1:** (right side) k 2, p 2 in ribbing to last 2 sts, k 2. **Row 2:** p 2, k 2 to last 2 sts, p 2. Rep last 2 rows twice more. **Row 7:** k. **On next row,** join T and p across. Continue in stockinette stitch (see pg. 10) for 5 more rows.

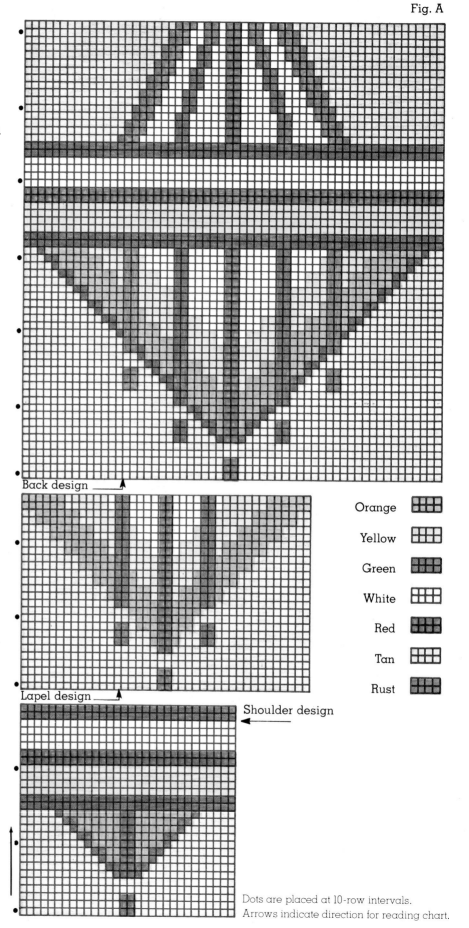

Fig. A

Back design

Lapel design

Shoulder design

Orange
Yellow
Green
White
Red
Tan
Rust

Dots are placed at 10-row intervals.
Arrows indicate direction for reading chart.

26 **Projects**

Dec 1 st beg and end next row. Rep this dec every 1" five times more. Work even on 74 (78, 82) sts until back measures 8½" from beg, ending with purled row. Join R and k 1 row. **Next 2 rows:** Rep ribbing rows as at beg of back. Continue in ribbing for 4 (4¼, 4½)", ending with 1ST ribbing row worked. K across next row. Join T and continue in stockinette stitch until 4½ (4¾, 5)" above R, ending with purled row.

Shape armholes: Rows 1 and 3: Dec 2 sts at each armhole edge. **Rows 2, and 4–10:** Dec 1 st at each armhole edge. Work even on rem 50 (54, 58) sts for 13 (15, 15) rows. Join G and k 2 rows. Join Y; work 4 rows stockinette stitch. Join RD, k next 2 rows. Join W; work 4 rows stockinette. Join G; k 2 rows. Join T; k 1 row, p 1 row. Dec 1 st beg and end of next 12 (13, 14) rows. Sl rem 26 (28, 30) sts to holder.

LEFT FRONT—Using size 9 straight needles and R, cast on 46 (48, 50) sts. Work ribbing as for back. **Next row:** k. Join T and continue in stockinette stitch for 6 rows.

Dec 1 st at beg of next row. Rep this dec every 1" five times more. Work evenly on 40 (42, 44) sts until front measures 8½" from beg, ending with purled row. Join R; k 1 row. Work in k 2, p 2 ribbing for 4 (4¼, 4½)", ending with wrong side row worked. K next row. Join T and continue in stockinette stitch for 2¾ (3⅛, 3¼)" above R, ending with purled row.

Shape neckline: k across to last 4 sts, k 2 tog, k 2. Rep this dec every k row 10 times more, and then every 4TH row 6 times. *At the same time* —when front measures same as back to underarm—shape armhole edge same as back. Continue working for 13 (15, 15) rows beyond armhole shaping. Work color sequence same as back. Continue in stockinette stitch on 11 (13, 15) sts for 10 (10, 12) rows; bind off.

RIGHT FRONT—Work same as left front, reversing shaping.

SLEEVES —(Make 2.) Using R and size 9 straight needles, cast on 52 (52, 60) sts. Work k 2, p 2 ribbing for 6 rows. K next row. Join T and continue in stockinette stitch for 11 (11¼, 11½)", ending with purled row. Dec 1 st each side of sleeve. Work 11 rows. Rep dec. Work 14 (16, 18) rows stockinette stitch.

Shape cap: Rows 1 and 3: Dec 2 sts each side of sleeve. **Row 2** (and all k rows): Dec 1 st each side of sleeve until 22 (26, 30) sts rem. Dec 1 st each side every 4TH row twice (18, 22, 26 sts). Join G; k 2 rows. Join Y; k 1 row. K, p, k next 3 rows, decreasing 1 st each side on p rows (14, 18, 22) sts. Join RD; k 2 rows. Join W; work 4 rows stockinette, decreasing 1 st each side on p rows (10, 14, 18 sts). Join G; k 2 rows. Join T; continue in stockinette stitch, decreasing 1 st each side of next 2 (3, 4) rows. Work 2 (2, 1) rows even; bind off.

POCKETS —(Make 2.) Using T and size 9 straight needles, cast on 25 sts. Work in stockinette stitch for 27 rows, and then in k 1, p 1 ribbing for 6 rows. Bind off.

BELT —Using size 5 straight needles and T, cast on 15 sts. Work in k 1, p 1 ribbing until belt measures 6'. Bind off in ribbing.

FINISHING —Join shoulder, side and sleeve seams. Set in sleeves.

Collar: (left side) With wrong side of sweater facing, join yarn to left front at beg of neck shaping. With size 9 straight needles, pick up and k 58 (58, 62) sts to shoulder seam. Work in stockinette stitch, decreasing 1 st each side of collar every row until 4 sts rem; bind off. Work right side of collar in same manner, beginning by picking up sts at shoulder seam.

Neckline trim: With right side of sweater facing, join R to bottom right front. Using circular needle, pick up and k 140 (160, 180) sts to center of back neck, including half the sts on back neck holder. K 2, p 2 in ribbing for 6 rows; bind off loosely in ribbing. Work other side in same manner, beginning by picking up sts at center of back neck. Join 2 sides tog at back neck.

Embroidery: With tapestry needle, embroider patt with duplicate stitch (see pages 14–15), using fig. A. Fold collar and steam-press. Tack collar to sweater body with tapestry needle and T. Using T, crochet two 5" chains. Tack at side seams midway in waist ribbing for belt loops. Sew pockets to left and right fronts 2¾" up from bottom edge and 4½ (4¾, 5)" in from center front edge.

Interlocking knitted motifs

Intertwined cables, stitch pattern

Stripes at side seam

Wall hanging

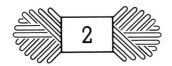

For explanation of project rating, see pg. 3.

Wall hangings have been the subject of a quiet renaissance in the last decade. The composition of interlocking knitted pieces uses only one stitch pattern. The design is by Cynthia Sterling Williams.

You'll need: Rug yarn—4 ounces *each* of rust (R) and blue (B); size 10 straight needles; tapestry needle; 2 weathered sticks 14" long or two 1"-diameter dowels 14" long; 8½" square of cardboard; nails and hammer to mount hanging.

GAUGE: 3 stitches=1 inch
4 rows=1 inch

SIZE: 10 by 26", excluding dowels and tassels

Knit wit

- Seed stitch is used throughout (see page 10).
- Increases are made by knitting two stitches in 1ST stitch of row.
- Decreases are made by slipping one stitch, knitting or purling one stitch (as required to keep seed stitch pattern), and passing slipped stitch over knitted or purled stitch.
- Roll each skein of yarn into two balls before beginning.
- Hanging consists of two identical pieces, one of which is inverted and woven through the other.
- To mount hanging, use one nail at each end of upper stick. (Nails should be long enough so hanging is slightly away from wall.)

Step by step

For key to abbreviations, see pg. 7.

FIRST PIECE—Cast on 10 sts with R. **Row 1:** k 1, p 1 to end. **Row 2:** p 1, k 1 to end. **Rows 3–12:** Inc 1 st in first st of each row until 20 sts. **Row 13:** Inc 1 st in first st, work next 9 sts, attach 2ND ball and work across last 10 sts. **Row 14:** Inc 1 st in first st, work next 9 sts; on 2ND side, dec 1 st in first st, work across. **Rows 15-23:** Working both sides at the same time, rep 14TH row 9 times (5 inc and dec in each side). **Row 24:** Work even across both sections. **Rows 25-34:** Dec at beg of 1ST section and work across. Inc at beg of 2ND section and work across that section. **Rows 35-45:** Working across all sts, dec 1 st at beg of each row until 10 sts rem. **Row 46:** Work even. **Rows 47-67:** Rep rows 3-23. **Row 68:** Work even across 1ST section; dec 1 st at beg of 2ND section and work across. Work even for 2 rows. Bind off both sections.

SECOND PIECE—Work same as 1ST piece, using B.

FINISHING—Invert 1 piece and weave through the other (see fig. A). Lash each section onto stick with tapestry needle, using appropriate color. Sew through each bound-off stitch. Make tassels: (Make 2 of R, 1 of B.) Wrap yarn 80 times around 8½" piece of cardboard (see pg. 17). Tie at top and cut bottom. Wrap 5 or 6 times with contrasting color yarn and tie off. Fasten onto stick at center of each section, with knots at back of hanging.

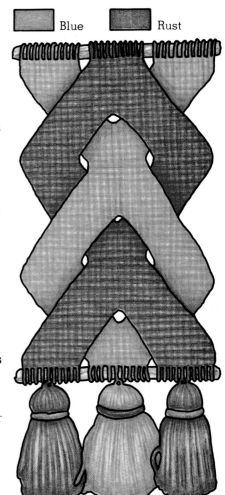

Blue   Rust

Fig. A

Detail of completed hanging

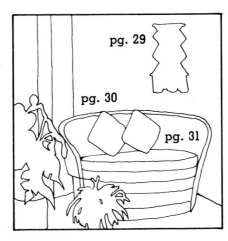

pg. 29

pg. 30

pg. 31

Aran pillow

See color photo, page 28.

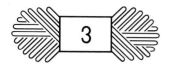

For explanation of project rating, see pg, 3.

Fishermen from the misty Aran Islands off the coast of Ireland keep warm in hand-knit sweaters known around the world as Aran sweaters. Knitted by village women, the sweaters are made in traditional stitch patterns such as cable, diamond, zig zag, and honeycomb — some of which have religious or cultural significance.

A small-scale introduction to Aran knitting, this pillow cover uses two stitch patterns in the Irish idiom. The cable section contains one knitted cable with a knitted cord woven throughout. The design is by Elizabeth Zimmerman.

For more examples of Aran stitch patterns, see the projects on pages 72—75 and 80.

You'll need: Knitting worsted — 8 ounces ecru; size eight 24" circular needle; 1 pair size 8 double-pointed needles; tapestry needle; 14 by 14" polyester or foam pillow; cable needle.

GAUGE: 4 stitches=1 inch
4 rows=1 inch
(in stockinette stitch)

SIZE: 14 by 14"

Knit wit

You'll need to know the following abbreviations and procedures to make this project:

- K 1b: Twist st by knitting into back of st.
- Rtw: Right twist. K 2ND st first from front, then k first st. Sl both sts off.
- Ltw: Left twist. Sl first st to cable needle and hold in front of work; k next st, then k st from cable needle.
- R over L cable: Sl 3 sts on cable needle and hold in front of work, k 3, k 3 sts from cable needle.*Replace these 3 sts on left needle and k them again; rep from *.
- L over R cable: Sl 3 sts on cable needle and hold in back of work, k 3. *Replace these 3 sts on left needle and k them again; rep from *. K 3 sts from cable needle.

Step by step

For key to abbreviations, see pg. 7.

CABLE CORDS — (Make 2.) Using size 8 double-pointed needles, cast on 3 sts. *K 3. Push sts to other end of needle without turning needle. Rep from * until cord measures 48".

PILLOW COVER — Cast on 114 sts using circular needle. Join, being careful not to twist. Work in stitch patt: **Rnd 1:** k 1b, p 2, k 12, p 1, k 1b, k 6, rtw, k 2, k 1b, p 1, k 1b, p 1, k 1b, k 2, ltw, k 6, k 1b, p 1, k 12, p 1. Rep from *. **Rnd 2:** *k 1b, p 2, R over L cable twice, p 1, k 1b, k 5, rtw, k 3, k 1b, p 1, k 1b, p 1, k 1b, k 3, ltw, k 5, k 1b, p 1, R over L cable twice, p 1. Rep from *. **Rnd 3:** *k 1b, p 2, k 12, p 1, k 1b, k 4, rtw, k 4, k 1b, p 1, k 1b, p 1, k 1b, k 4, ltw, k 4, k 1b, p 1, k 12, p 1. Rep from *. **Rnd 4:** *k 1b, p 2, k 12, p 1, k 1b, k 3, rtw, k 5, k 1b, p 1, k 1b, p 1, k 1b, k 5, ltw,

Fig. A

k 3, k 1b, p 1, k 12, p 1. Rep from *. **Rnd 5:** *k 1b, p 2, k 12, p 1, k 1b, k 2, rtw, k 6, k 1b, p 1, k 1b, p 1, k 1b, k 6, ltw, k 2, k 1b, p 1, k 12, p 1. Rep from *. **Rnd 6:** *k 1b, p 2, k 3, L over R cable, k 3, p 1, k 1b, k 1, rtw, k 6, rtw, p 1, k 1b, p 1, ltw, k 6, ltw, k 1, k 1b, p 1, k 3, L over R cable, k 3, p 1. Rep from *. **Rnd 7:** *k 1b, p 2, k 12, p 1, k 1b, rtw, k 6, rtw, k 1b, p 1, k 1b, p 1, k 1b, ltw, k 6, ltw, k 1b, p 1, k 12, p 1. Rep from *. **Rnd 8:** *k 1b, p 2, k 12, p 1, rtw, k 6, rtw, k 1, k 1b, p 1, k 1b, p 1, k 1b, k 1, ltw, k 6, ltw, p 1, k 12, p 1. Rep from *.

Rep rnds 1-8 until cover measures 14".

FINISHING — Weave back to front at top using tapestry needle; leave top side open. Insert pillow; sew open sides tog. Thread cords back and forth through double cables (see fig. A).

Ridged pillow

See color photo, page 28.

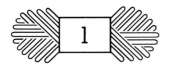

For explanation of project rating, see pg. 3.

The corrugated garter stitch used in this project makes a soft, thick pillow cover. For the striped side, choose any two colors that go well with your couch or favorite chair; for the back of the cover choose a solid color—ours is brown. The design is by Mary Walker Phillips.

You'll need: Knitting worsted — 4 ounces white (W), 8 ounces dark brown (B); size 8 straight needles; tapestry needle; 14 by 14" polyester or foam pillow.

GAUGE: 6 stitches=1 inch (corrugated garter stitch) 5 stitches=1 inch (seed stitch)

SIZE: 14 by 14"

Knit wit
- Carry colors loosely behind work.

Step by step

For key to abbreviations, see pg. 7.

FRONT — Cast on 82 sts with B. K 2 rows. **Corrugated garter stitch patt:** (Multiple of 8 plus 6 edge sts plus ½ rep of patt to balance patt). **Row 1:** sl 1, k 2 W, *k 4 B, k 4 W, rep from *, end k 4 B, k 3 W. **Row 2:** Same as row 1. **Row 3:** sl 1, k 1 W, k 5 B, *k 4 W, k 4 B, rep from *, end k 5 B, k 2 W. **Row 4:** Same as row 3. The difference in edge sts between rows 1 and

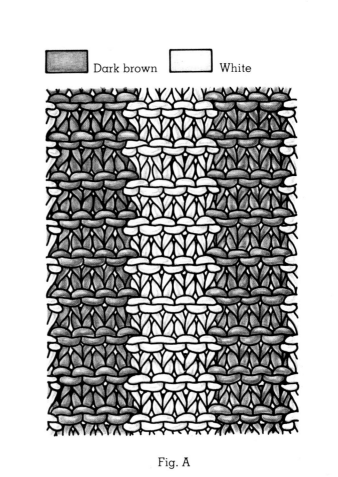

Dark brown   White

Fig. A

Detail of brown and white pattern

3 keeps edges from curling. Rep these 4 rows for patt (see fig. A) 20 times (40 white ridges). K 2 rows in B; bind off.

BACK — Cast on 69 sts with B. Rep seed stitch patt until back measures 13". **Seed stitch patt:** *k 1, p 1, rep from *, end k 1.

FINISHING — Block both front and back to 14". With right sides tog, sew the 2 pieces tog on 3 sides with tapestry needle. Turn right side out. Insert pillow; sew rem side.

Window shade

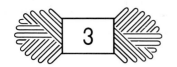

For explanation of project rating, see pg. 3.

Fishbones, spider webs, and primitive cellular shapes inspired this design. The herringbone lace stitch and seed stitch combine to make the tasseled shade, which can dress either the bottom or top portion of a window; you could adapt the design for a full window shade, too. The design is by Cynthia Sterling Williams.

You'll need: Cotton dress yarn — 12 ounces white; sizes 3 and 7 straight needles; tapestry needle; scissors; cardboard; ¼"-diameter wooden dowel, expandable curtain rod, or tension rod (length depends on size of finished curtain; dowel must measure 2" longer on each side than curtain); 2 brass cup hooks (optional).

GAUGE: 5 stitches=1 inch
8 rows=1 inch (in seed stitch on size 7 needles)

SIZE: 26½ by 19½", including loops and tassels

Step by step

For key to abbreviations, see pg. 7.

Curtain has modular units 3" wide. Each unit has 14 sts in 5 and 9 st patts. Measure window and areas you wish curtain to cover. Allow 4" for points and tassels and 1" for loops that go over rod or dowel. To calculate the number of sts you need across main body, round off window's width to nearest number divisible by 3. Divide by 3; multiply quotient by 14 and add 7 to obtain total number of sts.

TRIANGULAR POINTS —Using size 3 straight needles, cast on 7 sts. **Row 1:** k 7. **Row 2:** k 7. **Row 3:** k 6, turn, leaving 1 st on needle unknitted. **Rows 4, 6, 8, 10, 12:** k to end. **Row 5:** k 5, turn. **Row 7:** k 4, turn. **Row 9:** k 3, turn. **Row 11:** k 2, turn. **Row 13:** k 1, turn. **Row 14:** k to end. Cast on 7 sts.

For each point, proceed as in rows 1-14, casting on 7 sts at end of each 14TH row until you have 147 sts (or number of sts calculated for main body).

MAIN BODY—Use garter stitch (see pg. 10), seed stitch (see pg. 10), and double herringbone lace. Garter stitch forms border, seed stitch fills 5-stitch units, and lace stitch fills 9-stitch units.

Change to size 7 straight needles and work 1 row seed stitch, ending k 1. Work 2 more rows seed stitch.

Beg patt: Row 1 of curtain: seed st for 5 sts. Double herringbone lace for 9 sts (k 2 tog, * yo, k 2 tog, rep from *, end yo, k 1). Work seed st for 5 sts. Rep herringbone lace and seed st to end. Work each row as row 1 until curtain measures 18⅜", including points. Work 2 rows seed stitch across all sts; cast off as follows: **sl 1ST 5 sts to size 3 needles and work in seed stitch for 2" for curtain rod loop. Bind off**.

Using size 7 needles, bind off next 9 sts as follows: Attach new strand to next st and using double strand of yarn, bind off next 9 sts in seed stitch.

Rep from ** to ** for next loop. Continue working loops and casting off in same manner until all loops are completed.

FINISHING —Make 1 tassel, 3" long, for each point (see pg. 17). Using tapestry needle, sew each tassel to end of each point. Sew down loops using tapestry needle (see fig. A). Insert wooden dowel or curtain rod through loops; make sure dowel extends 2" on each side of curtain. Hold dowel in place with brass cup hooks at desired height, or place expandable rod inside window frame.

Knit wit
■ Spray starch will give shade more body.

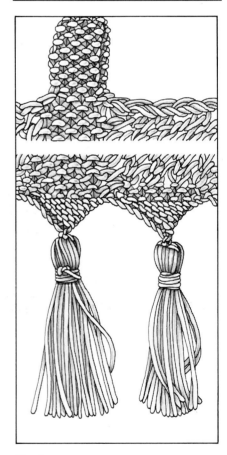

Fig. A

Ribbed V-neck

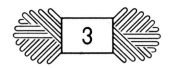

3

For explanation of project rating, see pg. 3.

Ridges of ribbing serve two purposes here — they add texture to this V-neck pullover and neatly camouflage the seams, making them barely visible. The design is by *Mon Tricot*.

You'll need: Sport yarn — 16 (20, 24) ounces cotton candy pink; sizes 4 and 6 straight needles; size four 24" circular needle; size 2 steel crochet hook; stitch holder; tapestry needle; safety pin.

GAUGE: 6 stitches=1 inch
17 rows=2 inches (on size 6 needles in k 3, p 3 ribbing, slightly stretched)

SIZE: Bust=34" (36", 38") Instructions are for size 34; changes for other sizes are in parentheses.

Knit wit
- Use extra stitch at each side of front and back as selvage when joining seams.
- Stripes: 6 rows garter stitch
          4 rows stockinette stitch

Step by step
For key to abbreviations, see pg. 7.

BACK —Using size 4 straight needles, cast on 101 (107, 113) sts. **Row 1:** (right side) k 4, *p 3, k 3, rep from * across, end k 4. **Row 2:** p 4, *k 3, p 3, rep from * across, end p 4. Rep last 2 rows for 4". Change to size 6 straight needles and continue ribbing until back measures 15½ (16, 17¾)" from beg or desired length to underarm, ending with row 2 worked.

Shape armholes: Bind off 3 sts beg next 2 rows. Dec 1 st each side of back every other row 3 times. Work even on rem 89 (95, 101) sts until armhole measures 7 (7½, 8)", ending with row 2 worked.

Shape shoulders: Bind off 12 sts beg next 2 rows and 11 (13, 15) sts beg next 2 rows; sl rem 43 (45, 47) sts to holder for back neck.

FRONT —Using size 4 straight needles, cast on 107 (113, 119) sts. **Row 1:** (right side) k 1, *p 3, k 3, rep from * across, end p 3, k 1. **Row 2:** p 1, *k 3, p 3, rep from * across, end k 3, p 1. Rep these 2 rows for 4", ending with wrong side row worked. Change to size 6 straight needles and work as follows: k 1, work next 18 sts in ribbing as established, k 69 (75, 81) sts, work next 18 sts in ribbing as established, end k 1. Continue working, keeping center sts in stripe patt (see *Knit wit*) and side 19 sts in established patt until front measures 2" shorter than back to underarm, ending with wrong side row worked.

Shape neck: (next row) Work across 53 (56, 59) sts in patt, sl center st to safety pin, attach 2ND ball to next st and finish row. Working both sides at same time, dec 1 st each neck edge every 2ND row 10 (11, 12) times, and every 4TH row 11 times. *At the same time —* when front measures same as back to underarm —shape armholes: Bind off 4 sts beg next 2 rows and 3 sts beg next 2 rows. Dec 1 st at armhole edges every 2ND row twice. Work even at armholes while keeping neck edge decs correct until armholes measure same as for back. Bind off for shoulder as back (no sts rem). Join shoulders.

LEFT SLEEVE —With right side of sweater facing, join yarn at left front armhole, 1 row above completion of armhole shaping. Using size 6 straight needles, pick up and k 35 (37, 41) sts to shoulder seam and 34 (38, 40) sts to top of dec at back armhole edge (69, 75, 81 sts). **Row 1:** (wrong side) p 3, k 3 across, end p 3. Pick up and k 2 more sts along armhole edge. **Row 2:** p 2, *k 3, p 3, rep from * across, end k 3.

Pick up and p 2 more sts along armhole edge. **Row 3:** k 2, *p 3, k 3, rep from * across, end p 3, k 2. Pick up and (k 1, p 1) 2 more sts. Continue in this manner to pick up 2 more sts at end of every row 4 times more, then 1 st each end once, keeping new sts in ribbing patt as established. Work even on 85 (91, 97) sts for 2".

Dec 1 st each side of sleeve. Rep this dec every 2" six times more. Work even on 71 (77, 83) sts until sleeve measures 17½ (18½, 19½)" from underarm. Change to size 4 straight needles and continue patt for 2¼"; bind off in ribbing.

RIGHT SLEEVE —With right side facing, join yarn at right back armhole edge. Using size 6 straight needles, pick up and k 34 (38, 40) sts to shoulder seam and 35 (37, 41) sts to top of dec at front armhole edge. Work same as left sleeve.

FINISHING —Neckband: Join yarn to first st on back neck holder. Using circular needle, rib off 43 (45, 47) sts from holder. Pick up and k 50 (54, 58) sts down left front neck edge, 1 st from pin, and 48 (54, 60) sts up right front neck edge (142, 155, 166 sts). **Next rnd:** p 3, *k 3, p 3 to center st. K 1, p 3, k 3 around. **Rnd 2:** Work in ribbing to 2 sts before center st, k 2 tog (or p 2 tog to maintain patt), k 1, k 2 tog, rib to end. Rep last rnd 8 (9, 10) times more. Bind off loosely in ribbing. Join side and underarm seams, reversing seam side on last 2½" of sleeves to turn back cuff.

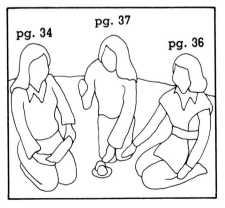

pg. 34   pg. 37   pg. 36

Ribbing along side seam

Zig zag jacquard pattern

One-piece back

Cache coeur

See color photo, page 35.

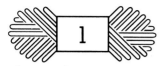

For explanation of project rating, see pg. 3.

Cache coeur means "hidden heart" in French, and the shoulder bands on this garment crisscross in front over your heart. The vest is held neatly in place by a purchased belt. The beauty of the cache coeur is its simplicity — there are no seams, buttonholes, or difficult techniques, so this project is an easy one for beginners (see fig. A). The design is by D. Armide.

You'll need: Sport yarn—8 ounces of blue; size 2 straight needles; size 3 steel crochet hook; purchased belt.

GAUGE: 6 stitches = 1 inch
17 rows = 2 inches (using double seed stitch)

SIZE: Bust = 34"
Adjust to any size by adding to length and width measurements.

Step by step

For key to abbreviations, see pg. 7.

BODY —Use double seed stitch patt throughout entire garment. **Double seed stitch patt: Row 1:** k 2, *p 2, k 2, rep from * to end. **Row 2:** p 2, *k 2, p 2, rep from * to end. **Row 3:** Rep row 2. **Row 4:** Rep row 1. Rep these 4 rows for patt.

16"

22½"

14"

90 sts

Starting from bottom of back, cast on 90 sts. Work even in patt until back measures 14".
Shoulder shaping: Inc 1 st each edge every 4 rows 12 times, keeping new sts in patt.
When back measures 22½", begin neckline: Work across 40 sts, attach 2ND ball of yarn and bind off center 34 sts. Work to end. Each shoulder band has 40 sts. Working both sides at same time, continue in patt until 7" above last inc.

Dec 1 st at outside edges every row until 30 sts rem on each shoulder band. Work even until 16" from last dec. Bind off 2 sts at beg of each row until 2 sts rem. Bind off.

FINISHING —Work 1 row reverse sc around all edges (see pg. 49).

Zig zag rag

See color photo, page 35.

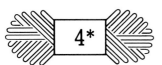

For explanation of project rating, see pg. 3.

Knitting can express an individual's feelings about nature, music, or color. This pullover's pattern was prompted by the designer's love of ragtime music. Here, an old song, *The Zig Zag Rag*, comes to life in a T-shaped sweater of 15 subtle colors. Knitted in one piece, the sweater fits loosely over a turtleneck or blouse. The design is by Astrid Furnival.

You'll need: Sport yarn — (refer to color key on page 38 for color definitions) 4 ounces each of A-O (Note: Extra yarn has been included to allow for size variations. Check with your yarn source about procedures for return of possible left-over yarn.); 2 size seven 29" circular needles; size F crochet hook; tapestry needle.

GAUGE: 5 stitches=1 inch
5 rows=1 inch

SIZES: Bust=34" (36", 38")
Instructions are for size 34; changes for other sizes are in parentheses.

Knit wit

- Use two strands of yarn throughout.
- Two colors (J and K) are mixtures and consist of 3 shades of fingering yarn (used as 1 strand). You can substitute variegated yarn instead of blending the shades.
- Be *sure* to check your gauge before beginning this project as the color pattern must be followed exactly if patterns are to match down side seams. To lengthen or shorten, you must add or subtract an identical pattern section on each side.

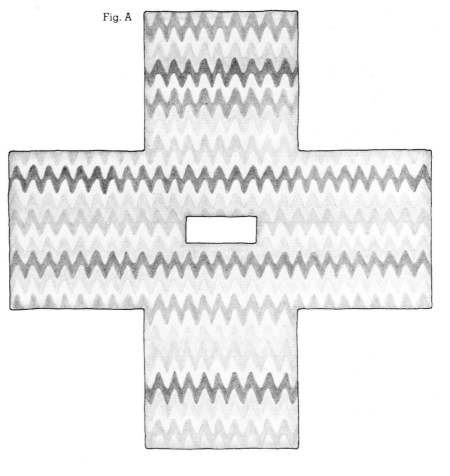

Fig. A

Step by step

For key to abbreviations, see pg. 7.

BODY —Work entire sweater in 1 piece, following the shaping in fig. A and the color design in fig. B, pg. 38.

Cast on 88 (92, 98) sts with A. Work in stockinette stitch (see pg. 10) until 16" from beg or desired length to underarm. Cast on 76 (80, 84) sts beg next 2 rows. Continue working in patt on 240 (252, 266) sts until the last row of 2 sts of N and 8 sts of L. **Next row:** k in patt across 101 (107, 114) sts, bind off center 38 sts. Attach 2ND strand of same colors to next st and finish row. Working both sides at the same time, work 8

rows. K 1 row M, casting on 38 sts above those previously bound off. Continue working in patt until 2ND half of sleeve is completed, repeating chart from B to C when you reach point A. Bind off 76 (80, 84) sts beg next 2 rows. Continue in patt on rem 88 (92, 98) sts until garment is completed. Bind off.

FINISHING —Join sleeve and side seams. Turn garment inside out. Using O, work 2 rows sc around neck and sleeve edges. Using A and B tog, work 2 rows sc around bottom edge of sweater.

(Continued on next page)

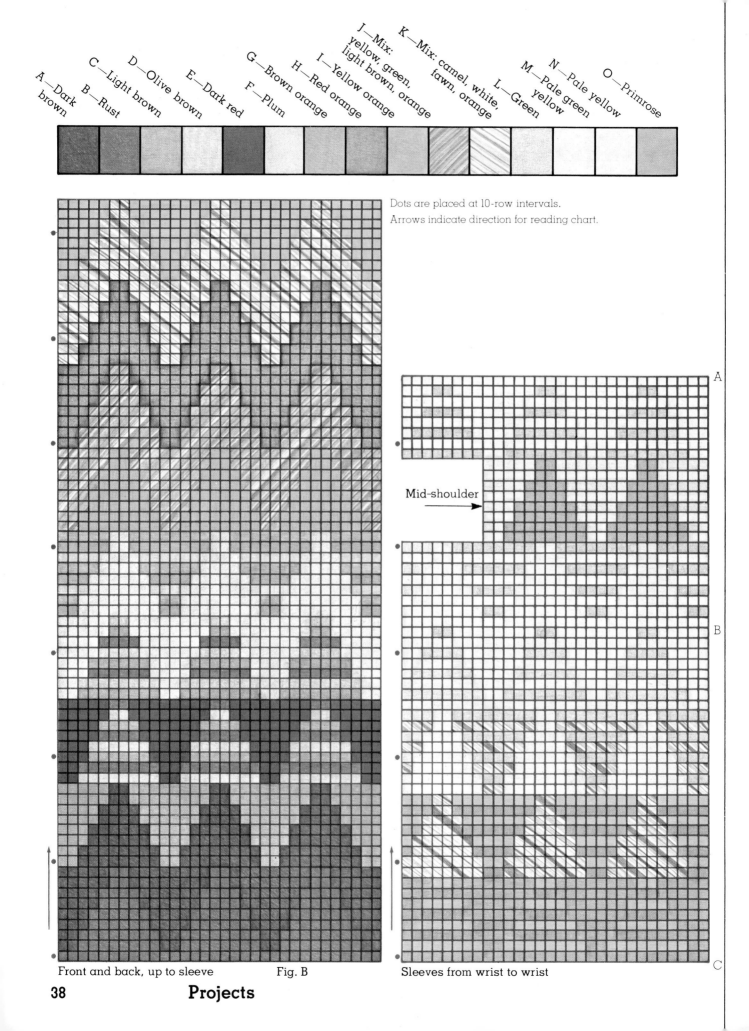

A—Dark brown
B—Rust
C—Light brown
D—Olive brown
E—Dark red
F—Plum
G—Brown orange
H—Red orange
I—Yellow orange
J—Mix: yellow, green, light brown, orange
K—Mix: camel, white, fawn, orange
L—Green
M—Pale green yellow
N—Pale yellow
O—Primrose

Dots are placed at 10-row intervals.

Arrows indicate direction for reading chart.

Mid-shoulder

A

B

C

Front and back, up to sleeve   Fig. B   Sleeves from wrist to wrist

Punchinello doll

See color photo, page 40.

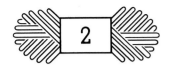

2

For explanation of project rating, see pg. 3.

Punchinello, the traditional comedy figure in Italian theater, was the spirited, colorful character that inspired the creation of Punch—of *Punch and Judy* fame.

Wearing the same happy face both front and back, this Punchinello doll is a cheery companion for a child. The design is by Sonja Pimentel.

You'll need: Rug yarn—4 ounces hot pink (P), 2 ounces *each* of magenta (M) and white (W); knitting worsted—1 ounce teal blue (B); sport yarn for trim—33' gold, 18' *each* of olive green, teal blue, orange, and hot pink, 9' scarlet, 5' magenta; fingering yarn for embroidery and hair—6' hot pink, 3' *each* of navy, kelly green, and scarlet, 1 ounce orange; sizes 8 and 9 straight needles; stitch holder; size G crochet hook; tapestry needle; 3' of 2"-wide cotton lace for ruffles; stuffing material (cotton or polyester).

GAUGE: 3 stitches=1 inch
9 rows=2 inches (using stockinette stitch with size 9 needles)

SIZE: Finished doll 15½" tall

Step by step

For key to abbreviations, see pg. 7.

FOOT AND LEG—(Make 2.) Using size 9 needles and P, cast on 24 sts. **Row 1:** p. **Row 2:** k 10, k 2 tog twice, k 10. Dec twice at center *every* row 5 more times until 12 sts rem. Work even until foot and leg measure 5½", ending with knitted row. Break off and place on stitch holder.

BODY—Working from the left, place right-hand 6 sts of left leg and left-hand 6 sts of right leg on size 9 needle. (Place rem sts on stitch holder for other side.) K 6, cast on 3, k 6. Work even on 15 sts for 5½". Bind off. Work other side the same way.

HEAD—**Row 1:** Using size 9 needles and W, working from the right, pick up and k center 13 bound-off sts at top of body. **Row 2:** p. **Row 3:** k. **Row 4:** p. **Row 5:** k to last 2 sts, k 2 tog, cast on 3 sts (15 sts). **Rows 6-11:** Work even. **Row 12:** p 2 tog, p across. **Row 13:** k to last 2 sts, k 2 tog. **Row 14:** p 2 tog, p across (12 sts). **Row 15:** k 2 tog, k across (11 sts). **Rows 16-20:** Work even. Bind off in p. Make 2ND piece, reversing shaping.

ARMS—(Make 2.) Work sideways with dropped sts. Using size 9 needles and P, cast on 12 sts. Work 3 rows stockinette stitch. **Row 4** (turn row): k 7, turn and p back. Continue in stockinette stitch, turning every 7TH row 3 more times. Work 2 rows even, ending with purled row (27 rows).

Bind off: k 1 pulling a 1½" loop, *drop next st, k and bind off next st very loosely (using first st on right needle), rep from * twice, drop next st, bind off rem 4 sts with normal tension. Pull out dropped sts.

HANDS—(Make 2.) Using size 9 needles and W, cast on 10 sts. Starting with p row, work 7 rows. **Row 8:** p 2 tog, p 1, p 2 tog twice, p 1, p 2 tog. **Row 9:** k 2 tog 3 times. **Row 10:** k 3 tog. Fasten off.

HAT—(Make 2 pieces.) Using size 8 needles and B, cast on 30 sts. Work in garter stitch (see pg. 10) 3 rows. **Rows 4–11:** Dec 1 st each end every row (14 sts). **Rows 12–14:** Inc 1 st each end every row (20 sts). **Rows 15–19:** Work even. **Rows 20–25:** Dec 1 st each end every row. Bind off rem 8 sts.

Garland: Using crochet hook and olive green, ch 40 (or enough to fit around narrow part of hat). Join with sl st to 1ST ch. *Ch 3, sc in 1ST ch from hook, dc, then sl st in same space (leaf). Sl st in next 3 ch. Rep from * back to beg. Break off.

Flowers: (Make 4 blue, 3 each gold, orange, and pink, 2 scarlet, 1 magenta.) *Ch 7, join with sl st to 1ST ch. Rep from * until 5 loops are completed. Break off.

FINISHING—Sew seams from outside starting with feet, then legs, body, and head, stuffing as you go.

With p side out, roll sleeves sideways so they are 2 layers thick and sew tog. Sew dropped st end to shoulders. Stuff hands and sew to wrists.

Sew hat pieces tog around sides and in 1½" from corners at bottom edges. Sew flowers to garland in irregular clusters and attach to hat.

Wrap orange fingering yarn around 8" book, leaving 30" tail. Cut through center and sew to top of head, catching face and nape of neck. Braid rem yarn, leaving 3' tail for embroidery.

Embroider face, using kelly green and navy for eyes, pink for cheeks, and scarlet for mouth (see photo detail, pg. 40).

Ribbon section attached to squares

Detail of face embroidery

Patchwork jacket

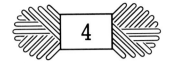

4

For explanation of project rating, see pg. 3.

Knitted squares of undulating colors form this loose-fitting jacket for a small child. A variety of ribbons are sewn onto the squares to complement the design. The modular format allows you to work on one square at a time instead of carting the whole project with you wherever you go. The design is by Marika Contompasis.

You'll need: Fingering yarn — 2 ounces *each* of dark blue (DB), medium blue (MB), light blue (LB), and yellow (Y); 1"- wide ribbon as follows: 15' medium blue, 8' gray, 7' *each* medium and dark blue plaid, and 5' purple; 3' lightweight knit fabric for lining; size 2 straight needles; tapestry needle; needle or sewing machine and thread for lining and assembling ribbons.

GAUGE: 8 stitches=1 inch
12 rows=1 inch

SIZE: Chest=24"
To enlarge sweater, use more strips of ribbon or wider ribbon.

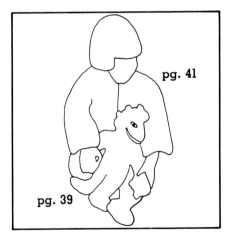

pg. 41

pg. 39

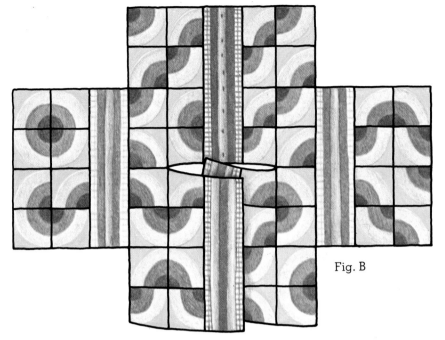

Fig. B

Knit wit

- Stockinette stitch used throughout (see page 10).
- Block each square by pinning to cardboard marked with exact 3 by 3" measurement. Spray with water and let dry.
- Use sewing machine for lining and ribbon assembly.

Step by step

For key to abbreviations, see pg. 7.

SQUARES — (Make 48.) Cast on 25 sts and work for 36 rows according to graph (fig. A). Sew tog in 6 units of 8 squares. Block by pressing units with steam iron, using pressing cloth.

RIBBONS — (Make 5.) Sew ribbons tog in 3 by 12" strips.

ASSEMBLY — Sew blocks of squares and ribbons tog as in fig. B. Trace jacket onto lining. Cut, allowing ⅝" seam allowances. Cut 2 panels for front overlap. Sew jacket tog at sides and neck opening as shown. Sew lining tog along sides and sleeves. Cut front opening in lining. Sew overlap panels to front edges. Place lining inside jacket, wrong sides tog, and baste raw edges. Trim away extra material and sew ribbon around edges.

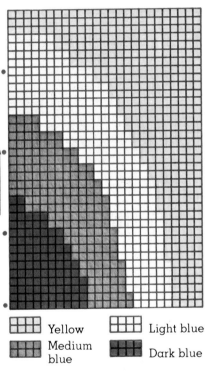

	Yellow		Light blue
	Medium blue		Dark blue

Fig. A

Arrows indicate direction for reading chart. Dots are placed at 10-row intervals.

Gold coil belt

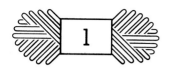

For explanation of project rating, see pg. 3.

Arabian sheiks secure their flowing head coverings with gold-wrapped coils. These exotic windings inspired the design of this belt, which uses coils knitted on a spool with a metallic-type yarn. The design is by Betty Erickson.

You'll need: Lurex fingering yarn —2 ounces gold; 3/16"-wide cotton cord (waist measurement times 3, plus 9"); braid fastener; rayon embroidery thread —12' *each* of purple, pink, and maroon; gold sewing silk or cotton thread; purchased knitting spool or homemade spool (empty thread spool with small finishing nails placed evenly around center hole; see fig. A); size 14 steel crochet hook; sewing needle; scissors; cellophane tape; large safety pin.

SIZE: Work coils to accommodate size of waist.

Step by step

For key to abbreviations, see pg. 7.

GOLD COILS — (Make 3.) Make small slipknot with lurex, leaving 4" tail. Place knot onto 1ST nail, dropping tail through center hole. Working clockwise, wrap yarn around each nail with each loop cross facing center of spool.

When you reach nail 1, carry yarn past outside of nails (not around nail as in cast on), lifting cast-on loop (nail 1) up over this yarn and nail (see fig. B).

Continue around spool, lifting each loop at base of nail over wound yarn and nail, creating next row of loops. After every few loop sts, pull tail and knitted coil downward through spool.

When you reach waist measurement minus 2" (with-

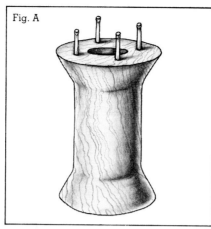

Fig. A

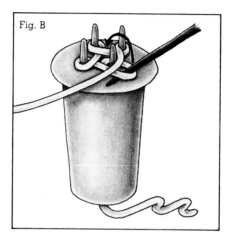

Fig. B

out stretching), cut yarn, leaving 12 to 18" in case you need to put coil back on spool to adjust length. Run yarn ends through loops on nail to cast off. *Do not* pull tight.

ASSEMBLY —Wrap end of cord tightly with narrow cellophane tape. Measure additional cord to waist measurement plus 1". Cut and tape added inch. Sl large safety pin lengthwise through taped end so that head of pin will lead cord through knitted coil. When all 3 coils have been threaded, measure coils again. Do not stretch knitting. (If cotton cords take up too much length, remove cords and replace knitted coils on spool and adjust.) Cut through taped ends, leaving 1/8" of tape to hold cording tog. Pull yarn ends tightly, enclosing cording in knitted coil. Cut yarn ends, knot, and thread back through cording to fasten.

FINISHING —St coils tog at ends with thread or sewing silk and baste in middle back of belt. At 4 regular intervals, wrap each coil separately, 1 with purple embroidery thread, 1 with pink, and 1 with maroon. Use needle to hide knot at beg and end of coils under wrapping on back of belt. Remove middle back basting. With gold sewing silk or thread, st through coils on either side of wrapping to keep coils tog. St on braid fastener with needle and sewing thread.

Knit wit

- To make an adjustable belt, use elasticized lurex yarn; eliminate cording and colored wrapping.
- To make a contour hip belt, make each coil slightly longer than the preceding one.

pg. 45
Scalloped scarf

pg. 44
Shoulder bag

pg. 42
Gold coil belt

Scalloped scarf

Shoulder bag

Gold coil belt

Shoulder bag

See color photo, page 43.

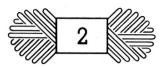

2

For explanation of project rating, see pg. 3.

Persian colors mingle with French motifs to make this timeless shoulder bag of rya yarn. The purse is long-wearing, and the lining prevents anything from falling out. The design is by Sonja Pimentel.

You'll need: Rya yarn — 3½ ounces *each* of tobacco (T), magenta (M), brick red (B), and light red (R); size 6 straight needles; tapestry needle; solid color or print purchased knit fabric, 23 by 18"; needle and thread to match fabric; scissors.

GAUGE: 5 stitches=1 inch
5 rows=1 inch

SIZE: 9½ by 8", excluding strap

Step by step

For key to abbreviations, see pg. 7.

BAG SIDE — (Make 2.) Cast on 45 sts with B. Attach R. Work vertical stripes as follows: k 2 B, *1 R, 3 B, rep from *, end 2 B. **On next row:** p 2 B, *1 R, 3 B, rep from *, end 2 B. Rep these 2 rows for 12 rows, ending with purled row. Break off B and R. Attach T. K 1 row with T. Attach M; work fleur-de-lis patt as follows: **Row 1:** p 2 T, *1 M, 3 T, rep from *, end 2 T.

Row 2: k 1 T, *3 M, 1 T, rep from *. **Row 3:** Same as row 1. **Row 4:** k 1 M, *3 T, 1 M, rep from *. **Row 5:** p 2 M, *1 T, 3 M, rep from *, end 2 M. **Row 6:** Same as row 4.

Rep these 6 rows until side measures 11" from point where T and M were added. Working patt as established, dec 1 st at each end of next 5 rows. Break off M. Bind off rem 35 sts with T only.

HANDLE — Cut 24 strands of B 50" long. Make 4-ply braid as follows: Divide strands into 4 groups of 6 strands each. (Each group of six = 1 strand.) Knot 1 end of the 4 strands tog; attach end to door knob or chair leg, or have someone hold the end. Hold 2 strands in left hand and 2 in right hand. Take outer strand in right hand behind and up between 2 left strands and back across inner left strand to right (see fig. A). Take outer strand on left back behind and up between the 2 right-hand strands and back across inner right-hand strands to left (see fig. B). Rep these 2 actions until handle is 40" long. Knot end.

ASSEMBLY — Steam-press bag sides lightly on both sides. With tapestry needle and T, sew both sides tog, right sides facing, with striped border at top of bag. Fold and sew down top border so that ¾" of border shows on outside. Sew handle to inside about 2" down so that finished length of handle is 36". Use purse as patt and cut 2 pieces purchased knit fabric for lining, allowing ½" seam allowance. Sew lining pieces tog, right sides tog, with needle and thread. Turn lining right side out and tack in place about 1" from top of bag. Turn bag right side out.

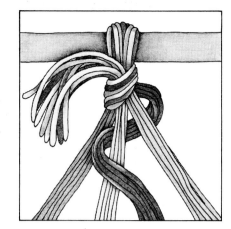

Fig. A

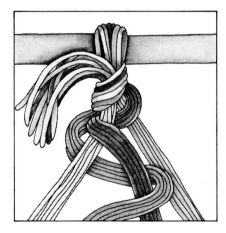

Fig. B

Scalloped scarf

See color photo, page 43.

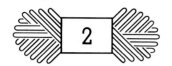

For explanation of project rating, see pg. 3.

Subtle shades of blues and greens highlight this scarf with its soft, graceful lines. The ends are flared and ruffled; colors are broken up by throw stitches, giving a lacy effect. To hold the scarf securely in place, one end passes through a slit. The design is by Jean Low.

You'll need: Sport yarn — 8 ounces light blue (B); fingering yarn — 2 ounces *each* of aqua (A), light green (G), and purple (P); size 7 straight needles; size F crochet hook; row counter.

GAUGE: 5 stitches = 1 inch
7 rows = 1 inch (using stockinette stitch and double-strand yarn)

SIZE: 9 by 72″

Knit wit

- Use double strands of yarn throughout: 1 strand blue with 1 strand green, aqua, or purple (alternating).
- Colors are always changed on the knit side.
- Increase and decrease rows are knit rows.

Step by step

For key to abbreviations, see pg. 7.

Cast on 90 sts with B and G. Work in stockinette stitch (see pg. 10) for 26 rows. Drop G. With B and A, k 2 tog across row (45 sts). Work in stockinette stitch for 15 rows more. Drop A. With B and P, inc 1 in each st by knitting in front and back of st (90 sts). Work even in stockinette stitch for 7 more rows. Drop P. With B and G, k 2 tog across row (45 sts). Work even in stockinette stitch for 9 more rows. Drop G. With B and A, inc 1 in each st across row (90 sts). Work even in stockinette stitch for 7 more rows. Drop A. With B and P, k 2 tog across row (45 sts).

Begin throw patt: k 1 row, making throw in each st by wrapping yarn around needle twice after inserting it in st. K st, catching and pulling both throws through (see fig. A). In next row, k each st, drop each throw (45 sts). Next row: k. (You will be on p side.)

*On k side, change colors and k. Maintain patt as established; work stockinette stitch for 25 rows; change color and work 1 row k, 1 row k with throw, 1 row dropping throw. K 1 row, change colors. Rep from * 10 times or until desired length is reached.

After 6TH rep, make slit: Beg 7TH rep in usual manner, but k 22 sts, drop those 2 strands of yarn and fasten in 2 more of same color, k to end. Continue in stockinette as before, working each side with its own double strand. After 26TH stockinette row, drop extra double strand and k across with 1 double strand. (See fig. B of completed slit.)

After 10TH rep, change color and inc 1 st in each st (90 sts). Work in stockinette stitch for 7 more rows. Change color and k 2 tog across row (45 sts). Work stockinette stitch for 9 more rows. Change color and inc 1 st in each st (90 sts). Work stockinette stitch for 7

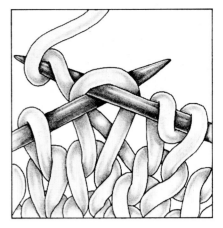

Fig. A

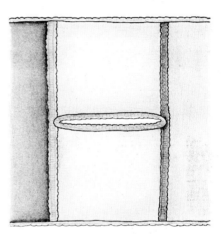

Fig. B

Detail of scarf slit

more rows. Change color and work dec row. Work 15 more rows stockinette stitch. Change colors and work inc row. Work 25 more rows stockinette stitch. Bind off.

FINISHING — Using A and B and crochet hook, sc 1 row around entire scarf. Crocheting in loose ends, sc 1 row around slit; crochet over loose ends. Reverse sc (see pg. 49) 1 row at both ends of scarf and around slit with A and B.

Side button closure

Chinese tunic

4*

For explanation of project rating, see pg. 3.

Slip into a shimmering Chinese tunic, a dramatic accent for an elegant evening. Small covered buttons fasten the tunic down one shoulder and side seam. The design is by Jani Fellows.

You'll need: Lurex fingering yarn —160 (180, 180, 200, 200) grams (not available in ounces) of dark brown (B), 120 (140, 140, 160, 160) grams *each* of copper (C) and gold (G); size 3 straight needles; size J crochet hook; 16 safety pins; 16 half-ball button molds, size 18; tapestry needle.

GAUGE: 8 stitches = 1 inch
14 rows = 1 inch

SIZE: Bust = 32″ (34″, 36″, 38″, 40″) Instructions are for size 32; changes for other sizes are in parentheses.

Knit wit
- Adjust length of tunic before decreases begin.

Step by step

For key to abbreviations, see pg. 7.

BACK —Cast on 135 (143, 151, 159, 167) sts B. Work in patt until back measures 5″, ending with patt row 2 or 4.

Stitch patt: (All sl sts as to p.)
Row 1: (right side) With B, k 3, *sl 1, k 3, rep from * to end.
Row 2: k 3, *wyif, sl 1, wyib, k 3, rep from * to end. **Row 3:** With C, k 1, *sl 1, k 3, rep from * to last 2 sts, sl 1, k 1. **Row 4:** with A, k 1, *wyif, sl 1, wyib k 3, rep from * to last 2 sts, sl 1, k 1.
Rows 5 and 6: With G, rep rows 1 and 2. **Rows 7 and 8:** With B, rep rows 3 and 4. Continue patt as in rows 1–4, changing colors every 2 rows as in rows 5–6 and 7–8, always following BCG sequence.

Mark with safety pin. Continuing patt, dec 1 st each side

and rep every ½″ eleven more times. Work even on 111 (119, 127, 135, 143) sts until back measures 12″.

Inc 1 st each side and rep every 1″ seven more times, keeping patt. Work even on 127 (135, 143, 151, 159) sts until back measures 19½″, ending with patt row 2 or 4.

Shape raglan: Bind off 4 (5, 5, 6, 6) sts beg next 2 rows. Dec 1 st each side every 4TH row 8 times, then every 2ND row until 41 (41, 43, 45, 47) sts rem. Bind off.

FRONT —Work same as back until 63 (63, 67, 69, 73) sts rem, ending with patt row 2 or 4.

Shape neck: k 2 tog, work 19 (19, 21, 21, 23) sts, bind off center 21, (21, 21, 23, 23) sts, work across. Work 1 row even, attaching 2ND ball to left shoulder. Dec 1 st each neck edge every other row 10 (10, 11, 11, 12) times. *At the same time,* make raglan dec at each side as in back until no sts rem.

SLEEVES —(Make 2.) Cast on 127 (127, 127, 143, 143) sts B. Work even in patt for ¾ (1, 1, 1, 1)″. Dec 1 st each side and rep every ¾ (1, 1, 1, 1)″ seventeen (14, 15, 14, 16) more times. Work even on 91 (97, 103, 105, 109) sts until sleeve measures 16 (16, 17, 17, 18)″ or desired length, ending with patt row 2 or 4.

Shape raglan: Bind off 4 (5, 5, 6, 6) sts beg next 2 rows. Dec 1 st each side every 4TH row 11 (12, 12, 14, 15) times, then every other row until 11 sts rem. Bind off.

FINISHING —Using back st (see pg. 16), sew right sleeve to front and back. Sew underarm seam and continue down side to safety pin. Sew left sleeve to back.

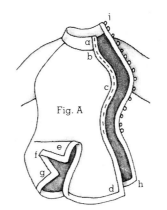

Fig. A

Neckband: (right side facing) Refer to fig. A. Join B at *a*. Work 1 row sc along neck edge, ch 1, turn. Work back in sc, ch 1, turn. Try on to check fit. Dec row: sc to 2 sts before 1ST raglan seam, pull up loop in next 2 sts, yo, pull through all 3 loops. Rep after next raglan seam and before and after next raglan seam (4 sts dec). Rep this row every other row until neck is as tight as desired. Work even until neckband measures 1½″. Fasten off.

Join B at back of neck. Work 4 rows sc from *i* to *f*, always ch 3 in corner st at *h* and *g*, and ch 1, turn at end of row. Work 1 more row from back of neck to *h* and from *g* to *f*. Fasten off. Join B at *a*. **Rows 1 and 2:** Work sc from *a* to *f*, always ch 3 in corner st at *c*, *d*, and *e*; ch 1, turn at end of row.

Attach safety pins to mark buttonholes: 1 at *a*, 1 at *b*, and 5 more evenly spaced to *c*, then 8 more at the same intervals down front. **Row 3:** sc, working buttonholes as marked; ch 1, turn at end. (Buttonholes: sc to safety pin, ch 3, skip 3 sc, sc to next pin.) **Row 4:** sc. Work 1 more row from *a* to *d* and *e* to *f*. Fasten off. Work 4 rows sc at bottom edge of sleeves, always ch 1 to turn.

Buttons: (Make 16.) With C, join with sl st in 1ST ch. Work 6 sc into circle, pull loop B through loop on hook, fasten off C and with B, *work 1 sc in 1ST sc, 2 sc in next sc. Rep from * 2 more times (9 sc). Put safety pin in last sc. *Work 2 sc in next sc, 1 sc in next sc, rep from * around, working 1 sc in last sc (12 sc). Work 1 sc in each sc. Insert button mold (with back on) into platter and work 1 sl st in every 2ND sc until mold is completely covered. Fasten off.

Block tunic lightly, being careful not to flatten patt. Sew on buttons along opening and at *f*.

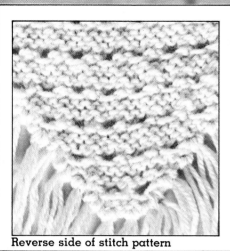

Reverse side of stitch pattern

Triangular shawl

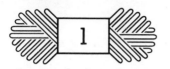

1

For explanation of project rating, see pg. 3.

A soft, lacy shawl, draped lightly over your shoulders, will keep you warm on cool summer evenings. This fringed triangular shawl uses one unique but simple reversible stitch pattern that creates a different effect on each side of the fabric. The design is by Helen Kisch.

You'll need: Knitting worsted — 20 ounces ecru; size eight 29" circular needle; size G crochet hook; 6½" square of cardboard; scissors.

GAUGE: 5 stitch patterns = 4 inches

SIZE: 72 by 35"

Step by step

For key to abbreviations, see pg. 7.

MAIN BODY—Cast on 3 sts.
Row 1: p, increasing 1 st at beg and end of row (5 sts). **Row 2:** k, increasing 1 st beg and end of row (7 sts). **Row 3:** k, increasing 1 st beg and end of row (9 sts). **Row 4:** *k 3 tog, keeping sts on left needle. *In same 3 sts*, k 1, k 2 tog. Rep from * to end. Rep these 4 rows for patt, increasing 1 st beg and end on 1ST 3 rows (*no inc on* 4TH *row*). Work 45 patts or to desired length. Bind off all sts.

FINISHING—Work 1 row sc on top of shawl. Do not turn. Work 2ND row reverse sc: work sc *left to right* (see figs. A and B).

Fringe: Make fringe, using method described in figs. C–E. Using 2 strands of yarn, attach fringes at regular intervals around sides of shawl.

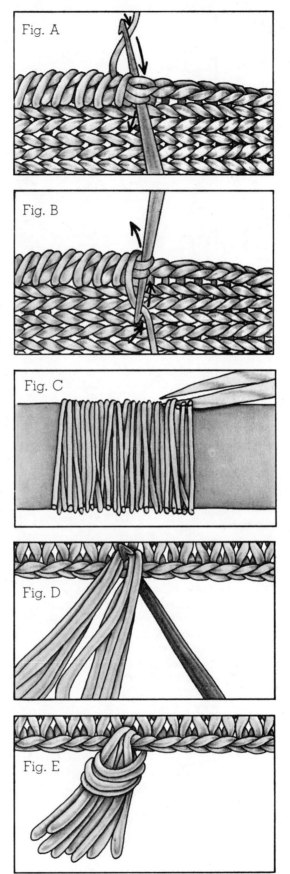

Fig. A

Fig. B

Fig. C

Fig. D

Fig. E

Capelet and cap

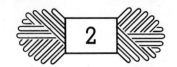

For explanation of project rating, see pg. 3.

The Parisian flair for fashion is evident in this Paris-designed capelet and cap ensemble. Both cap and capelet are made with the same simple stitch pattern. You begin at the side of each garment instead of at the bottom, as in most patterns. The scarf is part of the cape and wraps once or twice around the neck. The design is by *Mon Tricot*.

You'll need: Bulky yarn—40 ounces brick; size 13 straight needles; stitch markers; tapestry needle.

GAUGE: 3 stitches=1 inch
11 rows=2 inches
(Each ridge=2 rows)

SIZE: One size fits all

Knit wit
- Use garter stitch throughout (see page 10).
- See information on knitting short rows in **Knit wit** on page 64.

Step by step

For key to abbreviations, see pg. 7.

CAPE—Beg with end of scarf; cast on 22 sts and k even until scarf measures 25½". At left front edge, cast on 56 sts for cape. K 6 rows even on 78 sts.

Beg stitch patt: Row 1: Beg at lower left edge of cape k 50 sts, sl marker on needle, turn. **Row 2:** k 50 sts. **Row 3:** k 42 sts,

mark, turn. **Row 4:** k 42 sts. **Row 5:** k 30 sts, mark, turn. **Row 6:** k 30 sts. **Row 7:** k 16 sts, mark, turn. **Row 8:** k 16 sts. **Row 9 and 10:** k across 78 sts. Rep these 10 rows for patt 16 times more. K 4 rows on all sts. Work 10 rows patt 17 times more. K 6 rows on all sts. Bind off 56 sts at right edge and continue in garter stitch on rem 22 sts until scarf measures 25½". Bind off.

CAP—Cast on 34 sts and work as follows: **Rows 1 and 2:** k across all sts. **Row 3:** k 30 sts, sl marker on needle, turn. **Row 4:** k 30 sts. **Row 5:** k 26 sts, mark,

turn. **Row 6:** k 26 sts. **Row 7:** k 22 sts, mark, turn. **Row 8:** k 22 sts. Rep rows 1 through 8 ten more times. Bind off.

FINISHING—Using tapestry needle, sew cast-on and bound-off edges of hat tog. Weave yarn around opening in top of hat and draw closed; fasten off.

Cape shaping

Back view of cap and capelet

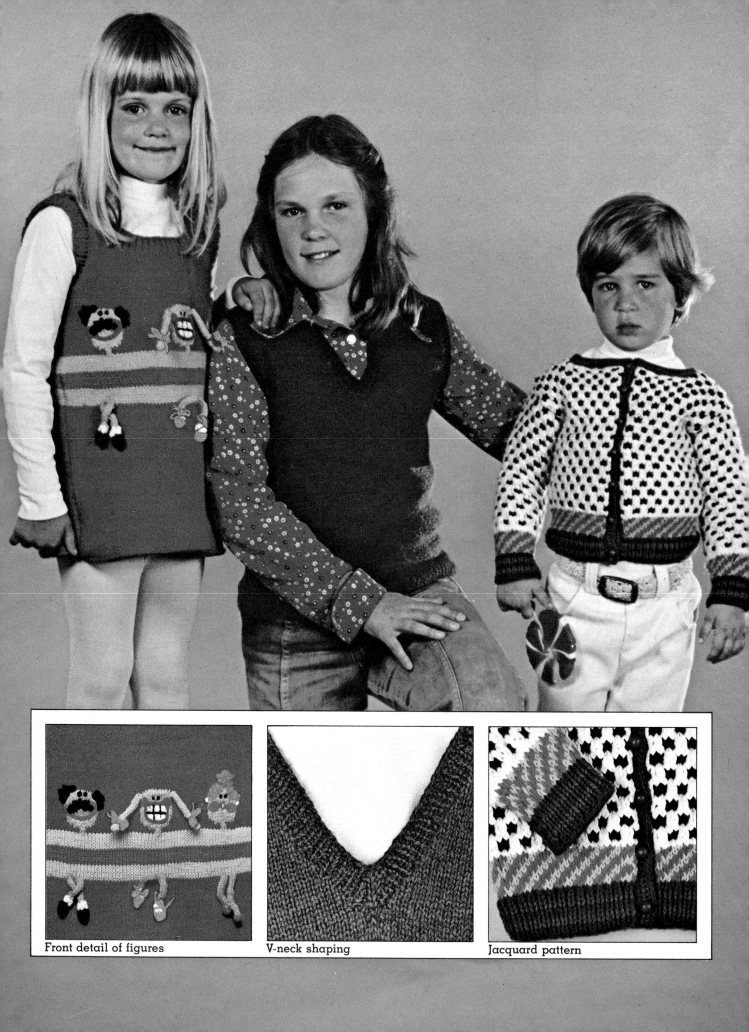

Front detail of figures

V-neck shaping

Jacquard pattern

Family jumper

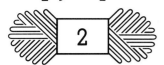

2

For explanation of project rating, see pg. 3.

The three-dimensional arms, legs, and smiling faces that leap from this knitted jumper would add a whimsical feeling to any child's garment. Arms and legs are knitted separately, and then attached; hair and embroidered features are added to the faces after the garment is completed. The three figures represent a family—mother, father, daughter —but can be personalized to represent any three people. The design is by Amy Bahrt.

You'll need: Knitting worsted — 8 (12, 12) ounces of red (R), 4 ounces *each* of gold (G) light pink (P), and purple (PR), 1 ounce *each* of bright pink, black, green, orange, and white; sizes 4 and 6 straight needles; size four 16" circular needle; knitting spool; size 14 steel crochet hook; stitch markers; 2 stitch holders; tapestry needle; 3 bobbins.

GAUGE: 5 stitches=1 inch
7 rows=1 inch

SIZE: Chest=26" (27½", 29")
Instructions are for size 26; changes for other sizes are in parentheses.

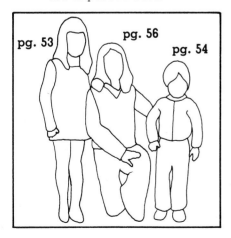

pg. 53   pg. 56   pg. 54

Back detail of figures

Knit wit

- Stockinette stitch is used throughout (see page 10).
- Jumper is planned for a 13½ (15, 17½)" length to underarm. Any adjustment should be made before decreasing begins.
- Wind bobbins before beginning.

Step by step

For key to abbreviations, see pg. 7.

BACK —Using size 6 straight needles and R, cast on 86 (90, 94) sts. Work in stockinette stitch for 1½", ending with knitted row. K next row on wrong side for hemline. Work even in stockinette stitch until 1½ (1¾, 2)" above hemline, ending with purled row. Next row: k 28 (30, 31) sts, sl marker on needle, k 30 (30, 32) sts, sl marker on needle, finish row. Dec row: *k to 2 sts before marker, k 2 tog, sl marker, sl next st as to p, k 1, psso, rep from * once, k to end (4 sts decreased). Rep dec row every 1½ (1¾, 2)" four more times. Drop markers and work even on 66 (70, 74) sts until 8 (9½, 11)" above hemline or desired length to waistline, ending with purled row.

Join G and work 6 rows stockinette stitch. Rep with PR and G. Join R. **Patt:** (row 1 of fig. A) k 11 (13, 15) sts, *join P, k 2 P, k 19 R*, rep from * to * once; join P, k 2 P, k 11 (13, 15) R. Continue working in stocki-

nette stitch until fig. A has been completed. Fasten off P. Work even in R for 1" above patt, ending with purled row.

Shape armholes: Bind off 6 sts beg next 2 rows. Dec 1 st each side of back every k row 6 times. Work even on 42 (46, 50) sts until armholes measure 3½ (3¾, 4)" above bind-off, ending with purled row.

Shape neck and shoulders: k 8 (9, 10) sts, sl center 26 (28, 30) sts to holder; attach 2ND ball R to next st and finish row. Working both sides at same time, dec 1 st each neck edge every k row 4 (5, 6) times. Work evenly on rem 4 sts until armholes measure 6 (6½, 7)". Bind off.

FRONT—Work same as back to armholes, ending with purled row. Bind off 6 sts beg next 2 rows. Dec 1 st each side every k row 3 (4, 5) times. Next k row: k 2 tog, k 7, k 2 tog, sl center 26 (28, 30) sts to holder, attach 2ND ball R to next st, k 2 tog, k 7, k 2 tog. Working both sides at the same time, continue to dec 1 st at armhole edges every k row 2 (1, 0) times more. *At the same time,* dec 1 st at neck edges every k row 3 (4, 5) times more. Work even on rem 4 sts on each side until armholes measure same as back. Bind off.

FINISHING—Join shoulder seams.

Armbands: Join R to right back armhole bind-off. With size 4

(Continued on next page)

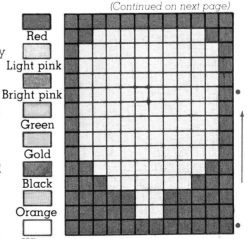

Red
Light pink
Bright pink
Green
Gold
Black
Orange
White

Arrows indicate direction for reading chart.
Fig. A Dots are placed at 10-row intervals.

straight needles, pick up and k 36 sts to shoulder seam and 37 sts from seam to end of right front armhole bind-off. **Row 1:** (wrong side) p 1, k 1 to last st, p 1. **Row 2:** k 1, p 1 to last st, k 1. Rep last 2 rows for ¾". Bind off loosely in ribbing. Make 2ND armband in same manner, joining R to front of left front bind-off.

Neckband: Join R to first st on back neck holder and k off 26 (28, 30) sts from holder to circular needle. Pick up and k 14 (16, 18) sts to shoulder seam, 17 (19, 21) sts to front neck holder, k off 26 (28, 30) sts from holder, pick up and k 17 (19, 21) sts to shoulder seam, 14 (16, 18) sts to beg. Sl marker on needle. Work in k 1, p 1 ribbing on 114 (126, 138) sts for ¾". Bind off loosely in ribbing.

Join side seams and st hem in place.

With knitting spool, (see pg. 42) make 3"-long tubes: 12 P, 4 G. Attach pairs of legs below stripes, centering at either side directly below each neck. Using duplicate stitch (see pg. 14), embroider shoes and socks as in fig. B and tack legs into desired positions. Attach braids to center head and tie bows. Embroider fronts and backs of heads and create hairstyles using French knots and other embroidery techniques (see figs. C, D, E).

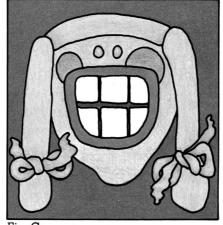
Fig. C

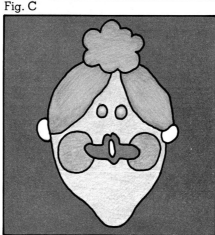
Fig. D

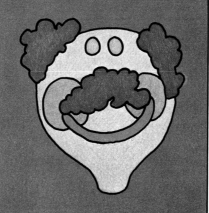
Fig. E

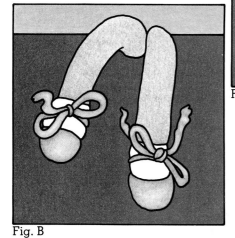
Fig. B

See color key, page 53.

Arrows indicate direction for reading chart. Dots are placed at 10-row intervals.

Child's cardigan

See color photo, page 52.

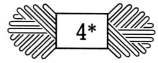
4*

For explanation of project rating, see pg. 3.

Vibrating colors and a jaunty, dotted pattern highlight this dashing child's cardigan. The colors are carried loosely on the inside to give the sweater a lush warmth. Tiny purple buttons fasten the front. The design is by Phoebe Fox.

You'll need: Knitting worsted — 3 (5, 7) ounces black (B), 5 (7, 9) ounces white (W), 1 (2, 3) ounces *each* of purple (P), turquoise (T), orange (O), and gold (G); sizes 6 and 8 straight needles; size G crochet hook; tapestry needle; seven ⅜" purple buttons.

GAUGE: 16 stitches=3 inches 8 rows=1 inch (in slip-stitch pattern, using size 8 needles)

SIZE: Chest=21" (23", 24") Instructions are for size 21; changes for other sizes are in parentheses.

Knit wit
- For increases and decreases, be careful to keep pattern dots aligned.

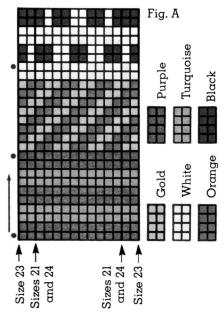
Fig. A

Purple Turquoise Black

Gold White Orange

Size 23
Sizes 21 and 24
Sizes 21 and 24
Size 23

Step by step

For key to abbreviations, see pg. 7.

BACK—Using size 8 needles, cast on 58 (62, 66) sts with P. Work 1 row in k 1, p 1 ribbing. Change to T and work 2 rows ribbing, then rep 2 rows with P, then T and P again.

Using O and G, work jacquard patt for 8 rows (see fig. A).

Change to size 10 needles and begin slip stitch patt. Sizes 21 and 24″ chest: **Row 1:** k with W. **Row 2:** p with W. **Row 3:** With B *k 2, wyib sl 2, rep from * to last 2 sts, k 2. **Row 4:** With B, *p 2, wyif sl 2, rep from * to last 2 sts, p 2. **Rows 5 and 6:** Rep rows 1 and 2. **Row 7:** With B, k 1, wyib sl 1, *k 2, wyib sl 2, rep from * to last 4 sts, k 2, wyib sl 1, k 1. **Row 8:** With B, p 1, wyif sl 1, *p 2, wyif sl 2, rep from * to last 4 sts, p 2, wyif sl 1, p 1. Size 23″ chest: **Rows 1 and 2:** Work as for sizes 21 and 24. **Rows 3 and 4:** Work as rows 7 and 8 of sizes 21 and 24. **Rows 5 and 6:** Rep rows 1 and 2. **Row 7:** With B, k 3, wyib sl 1, *k 2, wyib sl 2, rep from * to last 4 sts, wyib sl 1, k 3. **Row 8:** With B, p 3, wyif sl 1, *p 2, wyif sl 2, rep from * to last 4 sts, wyif

Back of cardigan

sl 1, p 3. Rep these 8 rows until 18 (20, 22) rows pattern dots have been completed.

Continuing in patt, work as follows: Work 1 row even. **Next row:** Work 14 (16, 18) sts. Bind off center 30 sts, work 14 (16, 18) sts. Work 2 (2, 3) additional rows patt dots. Bind off sts on wrong side with W. Work other shoulder the same way.

RIGHT FRONT—Using size 8 needles, cast on 30 (32, 34) sts with P. Work borders same as back. (Size 23: begin graph at sizes 21 and 24; end at size 23.) Change to size 10 needles. Work slipstitch patt as in back until 18 (20, 22) rows patt dots completed. Continuing patt, bind off 16 sts at neck edge (14, 16, 18 sts). Work 2 (3, 4) additional rows patt dots. Bind off on wrong side with W.

LEFT FRONT—Work same as right front, reversing patt and shaping.

SLEEVES—(Make 2.) Using size 8 needles, cast on 38 (42, 46) sts with P. Work borders same as for back. Change to size 10 needles. Working slipstitch

patt, inc 1 st each side on 10TH row, every 8TH row 3 (3,3) times, then every 12TH row 2 (3, 4) times more (50, 56, 62 sts). Work even until 17 (20, 23) rows patt dots are completed. Bind off on wrong side with W.

FINISHING—Join side and under-arm seams. Edging: (right side facing) **Rnd 1:** Using crochet hook and P, work 1 row sc along front and neck edges, making 3 sc at corners. Fasten off: **Rnd 2:** Mark 7 evenly spaced buttonholes (on right front for girl, left for boy) with top and bottom holes 2 sc from edge. Pull up loop to T (fasten off P), turn loop on hook, turn work. Work buttonholes on right or left front as follows: Work 1 sc in 1ST 2 sc, *ch 2, skip 2 sc, sc in each sc to next hole position. Rep from * to last 2 sc, sc in each sc. Fasten off T. **Rnd 3:** Pull up loop of P, ch 1. Work 1 sc in each sc, working 3 sc in each corner st and 1 sc in each ch 2 of every button-hole. Fasten off. Sew on buttons.

Versatile vest

See color photo, page 52.

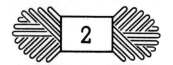

2

For explanation of project rating, see pg. 3.

A classic style is one that will remain in fashion much longer than any fad, and classic is the word for this design. The simple lines of the V-neck vest provide inspiration for a neat variation — the long-sleeved V-neck pullover. The design is by Jani Fellows.

You'll need: Knitting worsted — 2 (4, 8) ounces blue for sleeveless vest or 3 (8, 12) ounces blue for vest with sleeves; sizes 5 and 7 straight needles; size five 16" circular needle; size 1 steel crochet hook; stitch markers; stitch holder; tapestry needle.

GAUGE: 5 stitches=1 inch
6 rows=1 inch
(on size 7 needles)

SIZE: Chest=23" (24", 26") Instructions are for size 23; changes for other sizes are in parentheses.

Step by step—Vest

For key to abbreviations, see pg. 7.

BACK—Using size 5 straight needles, cast on 58 (60, 66) sts. Work in k 1, p 1 ribbing for 2". Change to size 7 straight needles and stockinette stitch (see pg. 10) and work until back measures 8 (9, 10)" from beg or desired length to underarm, ending with purled row.

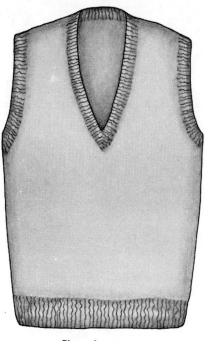

Sleeveless vest

Shape armholes: Bind off 4 (4, 5) sts beg next 2 rows. Dec 1 st at each armhole edge every k row 4 times. Work even on 42 (44, 48) sts until armholes measure 5½ (5¾, 6½)" above armhole bind-off.

Shape shoulders: Bind off 4 (5, 5) sts beg next 2 rows, 4 (4, 5) sts beg next 4 rows. Sl rem 18 sts to holder for back neck.

FRONT—Work same as for back until front measures same as back to underarm, ending with purled row.

Shape armholes and V-neck: Next row: Bind off 4 (4, 5) sts beg of row. K until 23 (24, 26) sts are on right-hand needle; k next 2 sts tog. Attach 2ND ball to next st and k 1ST 2 sts tog; k across rem sts. Bind off 4 (4, 5) sts beg next row. Working both sides at the same time, dec 1 st at each armhole edge every k row 4 times. *At the same time,* dec 1 st at each neck edge every ½" eight (8, 9) times more. Work evenly on 12 (13, 15) sts at each side until armholes measure same as for back; bind off for shoulders, same as for back.

ARMBANDS—(Make 2.) Join shoulder seams tog with tapestry needle. With right side of vest facing you, join yarn to beg of right back armhole bind-off. Using size 5 straight needles, pick up and k 32 (34, 36) sts to shoulder seam, 33 (35, 37) sts to end of 2ND bind-off. **Row 1:** (wrong side) p 1, k 1 across all sts, end p 1. **Row 2:** k 1, p 1 across all sts, end k 1. Rep these 2 rows until band measures ¾"; bind off loosely in ribbing. Make 2ND armband in same manner.

NECKBAND—Join yarn to 1ST st on back neck stitch holder. K off sts from back neck holder to circular needle; pick up and k 36 (38, 40) sts down left neck edge to center front. Sl marker on needle. Pick up and k 1 from center; sl marker on needle. Pick up and k 37 (39, 41) sts to top of right shoulder; sl marker on needle to indicate beg of rnds. **Rnd 1:** k 1, p 1 in ribbing to 2 sts before 1ST "V" marker; k 2 tog, sl marker, k center st, sl marker, k 2 tog, p 1, k 1 in ribbing to last st, p 1. Rep last rnd until border measures ¾"; bind off loosely in ribbing. Join side seams.

Pullover

Step by step—Pullover

For key to abbreviations, see pg. 7.

BACK—Work back same as vest to underarm, ending with purled row.

Shape armholes and V-neck: Bind off 2 (2, 3) sts beg next 2 rows. Dec 1 st each side every k row twice. Work even on 50 (52, 56) sts until armholes measure 4¾ (5½, 5¾)" above bind-off.

Shape shoulders: Bind off 4 (5, 5) sts beg next 2 rows, 4 (5, 5) sts beg next 2 rows, and 4 sts beg next 4 rows. Sl rem 18 (18, 20) sts to holder for back neck.

FRONT—Work same as back to underarm, ending with purled row. Shape armholes and neck: Bind off 2 (2, 3) sts beg next row. K until 21 (22, 23) sts are on right needle; k next 2 sts tog. Attach 2ND ball to next st; k next 2 sts tog; k across rem sts. Complete armhole shaping same as back. *At the same time*, rep neck edge dec every ½" eight (8, 9) times more. Shape shoulders same as for back when armholes measure same as back.

SLEEVES—(Make 2.) Using size 5 straight needles, cast on 30 (32, 34) sts. Work in k 1, p 1 ribbing for 2". Change to size 7 straight needles and stockinette stitch. Inc 1 st each side of sleeve next row and then every 1½" four (5, 6) times more. Work even on 40 (44, 48) sts until sleeve measures 9½ (10½, 12)" or desired length to underarm, ending with purled row.

Shape cap: Bind off 2 (2, 3) sts beg next 2 rows. Dec 1 st each side of sleeve every row 4 times, then every k row 3 (4, 4) times. Bind off 3 sts beg next 4 rows; bind off rem 10 (12, 14) sts.

FINISHING—Join shoulder, side and sleeve seams. Set sleeves into armholes. Work neckband in same manner as for sleeveless vest.

Sporty poncho

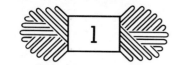

1

For explanation of project rating, see pg. 3.

Much like a Mexican sarape, this comfortable poncho slips easily over your head and is perfect for a walk on the beach. The shape is rectangular with a rectangular neck opening in the center of the garment. There are no buttons or seams and no increases or decreases. Only two stitch patterns—stockinette and garter—are used. The design is by *Mon Tricot*.

You'll need: Bulky yarn—44 ounces ecru; size 10 straight needles; stitch holder.

GAUGE: 4 stitches=1 inch
11 rows=2 inches

SIZE: One size fits all

Step by step

For key to abbreviations, see pg. 7.

FRONT—Cast on 148 sts. Work in garter stitch (see pg. 10) for 2". Keeping 9 sts at each side in garter stitch for border, work center 130 sts in stockinette stitch (see pg. 10) until work measures 22½" from beg.

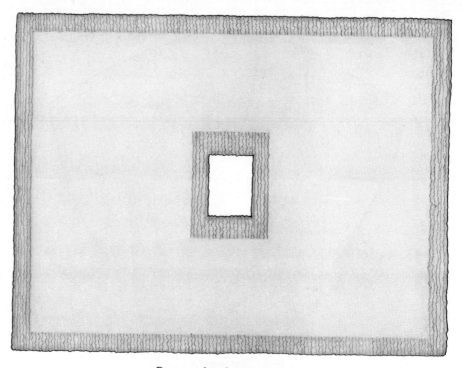

Rectangular shape of poncho

Shape front neck border: Row 1: (right side) k. **Row 2:** k 9, p 41, k 48, p 41, k 9. Rep these 2 rows until neck border measures 2".

Shape neck: Row 1: k 61 sts, sl on stitch holder, bind off center 26 sts, k 61 sts. **Row 2:** k 9, p 41, k 11. Continue working on these 61 sts, keeping 11 sts at neck border and 9 sts at side in garter stitch. When work measures 4", sl left side to stitch holder, join yarn to right side; work same as left side.

Shape back neck border: k 61, cast on 26, k 61 from holder. Work same as front neck border until back neck border measures 2".

BACK—Continue in stockinette stitch, keeping 9 sts at each side in garter stitch for border, until work measures 51½". Work bottom border in garter stitch for 2". Bind off.

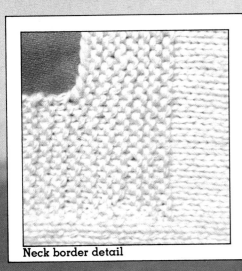

Neck border detail

Belt bag

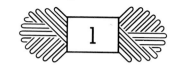

For explanation of project rating, see pg. 3.

This knitted belt bag works equally well as a coin purse or a golf tee holder; or use it to carry your lipstick and comb. Use any scrap yarn to make the bag; seeds, shells, leather, coins, or other small found objects serve as a weight for the purse flap. The design is by Joyce Scott.

You'll need: Knitting worsted — 2 ounces orange, ½ ounce tan; size 7 straight needles; size E crochet hook; 1 large and 1 medium button; 1 small bead (or any combination desired of buttons, beads, and leather to weight flap); 20 by 6" piece purchased knit fabric; sewing needle and thread to match fabric; scissors; pins; 3 stitch holders.

GAUGE: 5 stitches = 1 inch

SIZE: 5 by 8"

Step by step

For key to abbreviations, see pg. 7.

BACK —Cast on 25 sts of orange. Work in stockinette stitch (see pg. 10) until back measures 5¾", ending with purled row. Next row: p across 20 sts and sl to stitch holder. P every row on rem 5 sts for 4½" (or as required to accommodate belt). Sl sts to holder. Skip center 15 sts. Join yarn to next st and complete 2ND belt loop same as 1ST. Sl to holder.

FLAP —Sl center 15 sts from holder to needle. P every row until flap measures 4¾". Bind off.

FRONT —Sl sts from 1ST belt loop onto needle. Cast on 15 sts. Sl sts from 2ND belt loop onto needle. Work all 25 sts in stockinette stitch until front measures 5¾". Bind off.

Belt bag detail

ASSEMBLY —Fold bag in half with p side out. Tuck in all ends; line up back and front sides. Crochet seams, starting at bottom of 1ST belt loop and working to bottom of 2ND belt loop, using sc on right side.

CROCHET TRIM —With tan, work 1 row sc around belt loops and 2 rows sc around outer edge and flap from wrong side.

LINING —Measure width and length of purse; double length and add ½" seam allowance to width and total length. Cut purchased knit fabric to measurements. Fold fabric in half lengthwise. With sewing needle and thread, join sides. Tuck lining inside bag. Sew down excess of top edge and tack lining into bag. (Lining should ease into bag.)

DECORATIVE FLAP WEIGHT —With sewing needle and thread, sew buttons, beads, or other objects to bottom center of flap.

Knit wit
- Purl side is right side.
- Knit belt loops larger or smaller, to fit your belt.

Toasty mittens

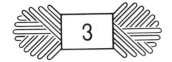

For explanation of project rating, see pg. 3.

Knitters in cold climates will ply their craft to good advantage when they make these warm woolen mittens. Vary the colors of the stripes on the backs of the mittens to complement your favorite ski or bicycle outfit. The design is by Rosalie Carl.

You'll need: Bulky weight yarn — 4 (6, 6) ounces dark brown (DB), 1 ounce *each* of beige (B) and ecru (E); size 3 double-pointed needles; stitch holder; stitch marker.

GAUGE: 9 stitches=2 inches
6 rows=1 inch

SIZE: Child's palm width=6½" (woman's=7½"; man's=9") Instructions are for child's mittens; changes for other sizes are in parentheses.

Step by step

For key to abbreviations, see pg. 7.

RIGHT-HAND MITTEN — Cast on 32 (36, 40) sts with DB — 8 (9, 10) sts each on needles 1 and 2, and 16 (18, 20) sts on needle 3. Join, being careful not to twist sts. Work in k 2, p 2 ribbing for 3 (3½, 4)".

Thumb shaping: Change to stockinette stitch (see pg. 10).

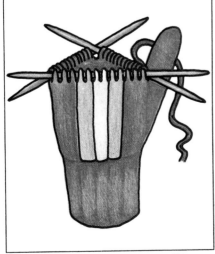

Working mittens on three needles

K 1 rnd. Start inc for thumb on needle 1. **Rnd 1:** Inc 1 st in first st, k 1, inc 1 st in next st, k around. **Rnd 2:** k. **Rnd 3:** k 18 (20, 22) sts DB across palm (needles 1 and 2). On patt side (needle 3), k as follows: 2 (3, 4) DB, 4 B, 4 E. Attach 2ND ball B and k 4 sts, k 2 (3, 4) DB. Carry DB loosely across back (wrong side), twisting it once around each color as new color is worked. Continue color stripes each rnd on needle 3. **Rnd 4:** (needle 1) Inc 1 st in first st, k 3, inc 1 st in next st, k around. K 2 rnds. Continue to inc 2 sts for thumb every 3RD rnd (with 2 sts more between increases) 3 (4, 5) more times. Sl 10 (12, 14) thumb sts to stitch holder or strand of yarn. Cast on 2 sts over thumb. K even for 2 (3, 3½)" for hand, continuing stripes on needle 3.

Top shaping: Keeping beg of rnds in same place, divide sts to have same number of sts across palm (needles 1 and 2) as on patt side — 17 (19, 21) sts each side. Continuing stripes, dec as follows: (Start with needle 1.) *k 1, sl 1, k 1, psso, k to end. Needle 2: k to within 3 sts from end, k 2 tog, k 1. Needle 3: k 1, sl 1, k 1, psso, k to 3 sts from end and k 2 tog, k 1. Work 1 rnd even. Rep from * until 14 (18, 22) sts rem. Join front to back.

Thumb: Sl sts of thumb to 2 needles. Pick up 2 cast-on sts plus 1 st each side of cast-on sts on 3RD needle. K around 14 (16, 18) thumb sts for 1 rnd. Dec 1 st beg of 1ST and end of 2ND needle next 2 rnds. K even on 10 (12, 14) sts for 1 (1½, 2)". K 2 tog all around. Thread yarn through rem sts; draw tight. Fasten off.

LEFT-HAND MITTEN — Work same as right-hand mitten but start thumb on opposite side.

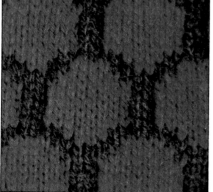

Honeycomb color pattern

Short row shaping

Tricolor pattern

Honeycomb hat

3

For explanation of project rating, see pg. 3.

A honeycomb pattern adds a bit of personality to this Tyrolean-style hat. To give the brim additional support, use hat wire, available at most craft shops. The design is by Joyce Carlo.

You'll need: Sport yarn—8 ounces copper (C), 4 ounces brown (B); size three double-pointed needles; stitch markers; hat wire; size G crochet hook; tapestry needle.

GAUGE: 7 stitches= 1 inch
8 rows= 1 inch

SIZE: Head circumference= 22" (23", 24")
Instructions are for 22" head size; changes for other sizes are in parentheses.

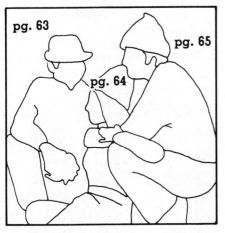

pg. 63
pg. 65
pg. 64

White squares=Copper Brown Fig. A

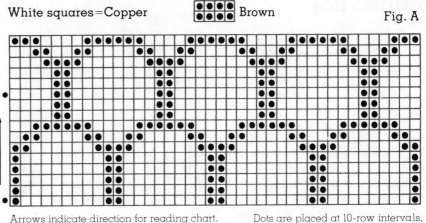

Arrows indicate direction for reading chart.   Dots are placed at 10-row intervals.

Knit wit
- Use contrasting marker to indicate beginning of rounds.

Step by step

For key to abbreviations, see pg. 7.

BRIM—Cast on 220 (230, 240) sts with C. Join, being careful not to twist. Working around in stockinette stitch with B and C, work patt rnd 1 (see fig. A). Place markers in patt rnd 2 as follows: 1 after 25 (30, 35) sts, 1 after next 60 sts, 1 after next 50 sts, 1 after next 60 sts, and 1 after next 25 (30, 35) sts.
Rnd 3: Dec (k 2 sts tog) after markers. **Rnd 4:** Dec (k 2 tog) before markers. Continue to dec in this manner until 130 (140, 150) sts rem.

HAT BODY— Work even in patt until hat body and brim measure 7" from beg. Using C, k 1 rnd without patt. Bind off loosely.

BRIM LINING—Cast on 220 (230, 240) sts with C. Work as for brim. Work 2 more rnds with no dec. Bind off loosely.

CROWN—(Make 2). Cast on 20 (24, 28) sts with C. Working in stockinette stitch, inc 1 st each side in 1ST rnd, then every other

rnd until there are 34 (42, 50) sts. Place marker. Work 2½ (3, 3½)" even. Dec 1 st each side every other rnd until 20 (24, 28) sts rem. Bind off.

FINISHING—With tapestry needle and matching yarn, join back seams. Join back seam of brim lining. Press seams. Stitch brim and brim lining at bottom. Insert hat wire into seam of brim and brim lining. Slipstitch wire in place. Place crown and crown lining wrong sides tog; st into top of hat body. Steam-press entire hat.

Striped hat

See color photo, page 62.

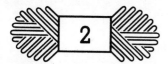

For explanation of project rating, see pg. 3.

If you're a beginner who wants to learn multicolor knitting, here's a project that will give you a pleasant introduction to this interesting technique. The tapering top of the hat results from a special technique of increasing— "short rows." The design is by Barbara Walker.

You'll need: Knitting worsted —
1 ounce *each* of magenta (M), orange (O), tan (T), and light blue (B); size 6 straight needles; tapestry needle.

GAUGE: 5 stitches=1 inch
10 rows=1 inch

SIZE: One size fits all

Striped hat

Step by step

For key to abbreviations, see pg. 7.

HAT BODY—With B, cast on 41 sts. K 1 row. Join T. **Rows 1 and 2:** With T, k 38; turn, k to end. Join O. **Rows 3 and 4:** With O, k 36; turn, k to end. Join M. **Rows 5 and 6:** With M, k 34; turn, k to end. **Rows 7 and 8:** With B, k 32; turn, k to end. **Rows 9 and 10:** With T, k 30; turn, k to end. **Rows 11 and 12:** With O, k 28; turn, k to end. **Rows 13 and 14:** With M, k 26; turn, k to end. **Rows 15 and 16:** With B, k across row.

These 16 rows make 1 segment of the cap. Work until there are 11 segments. End last segment with row 15.

FINISHING—Join sts of last row into cast-on edge. Draw short side edges tog at center. Thread with yarn; fasten off yarn on wrong side.

Knit wit

- When changing colors, draw new strand firmly up behind other 3 strands with right side of work facing you.
- Knitting short rows is a method of increasing the total number of rows. This has the effect of a dart and increases the surface area of the knitted fabric. Use short rows to shape a garment; you can flare an outside edge or inside section. Knit short rows by turning your work before knitting completely across a row. Work back to the beginning of the row. Repeat this process to increase the desired number of rows.
- To prevent holes when turning short rows (as in row 1), sl 1 wyif; pass yarn to back, return the sl st to left needle. Turn work; wyib between needles, continue knitting.
- *Note this optional procedure that gives cap a neater edge:* Pick up strands passed in previous short rows from front. Place them on left needle. K tog through back loops with sts around which they were passed (see fig. A).

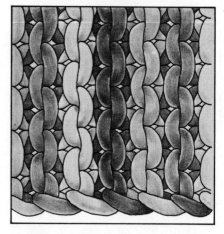

Fig. A

Mosaic pattern hat

See color photo, page 62.

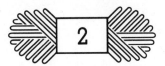

For explanation of project rating, see pg. 3.

Blocks of alternating colors create the mosaic pattern of this cuffed hat. Vary the colors to match your cold-weather outfits. The design is by Barbara Walker.

You'll need: Knitting worsted — 2 ounces *each* of royal blue (B), yellow (Y), and red (R); size six straight needles; size six 16" circular needle; tapestry needle; stitch marker.

GAUGE: 5 stitches = 1 inch
8 rows = 1 inch

SIZE: One size fits all

Mosaic pattern hat

Step by step

For key to abbreviations, see pg. 7.

HAT BODY — Using B, cast on 8 sts with size 6 straight needles. Chart on this page (fig. A) shows segment of color pattern

⊠⊠⊠⊠ Royal blue	◥◥◥◥ Yellow	●●●● Red	Fig. A

Arrows indicate direction for reading chart. Dots are placed at 10-row intervals.

worked as follows: **Row 1:** With B, k across row. This is the right side. **Row 2:** p 1, inc 1 st in each of next 6 sts, p 1 (14 sts). Join R. **Row 3:** (Begin chart.) With R, k 1, *sl 2 wyib, k 4; rep from *, k 1. **Row 4:** p 1, *p 4, sl 2 wyif; rep from *, p 1. **Row 5:** With B, k 1, *k 4, sl 2 wyib; rep from *, k 1. **Row 6:** p 1, *sl 2 wyif, p 4; rep from *, p 1. **Row 7:** With R, k across row. **Row 8:** p 1, inc 12 times, p 1 (26 sts). Join Y. **Rows 9 and 10:** With Y, rep rows 3 and 4. **Rows 11 and 12:** With R, rep rows 5 and 6. **Row 13:** With Y, k across row. **Row 14:** p 1, inc 24 times, p 1 (50 sts). **Rows 15 and 16:** With B, rep rows 3 and 4. **Rows 17 and 18:** With Y, rep rows 5 and 6. **Row 19:** With B, k across row. **Row 20:** With B, p 1, *p 1, inc; rep from * 23 times; p 1 (74 sts). **Rows 21–25:** Rep rows 3–7. **Row 26:** With R, p 1, *p 2, inc; rep from * 23 times, p 1 (98 sts). **Rows 27–31:** Rep rows 9–13. **Row 32:** With Y, p 1, *p 7, inc; rep from * 11 times, p 1 (110 sts). **Rows 33–37:** Rep rows 15–19. **Row 38:** With B, p across row.

Rep rows 3–20 twice more *without* further increasing. Work rows 8, 14, 20 as plain p rows. Break off R and Y. Place sts on circular needle. With tapestry needle, join center back seam.

RIBBING — With B, *p 2 tog, p 1, k 2; rep from * (88 sts). Sl marker on needle to mark rnds. Continue in p 2, k 2 ribbing in rnds until length of ribbed cuff measures 2½". Bind off loosely.

Knit wit

■ To increase on wrong side, insert right needle downward into purled head of stitch below first stitch on left needle. Purl; then purl first stitch (see fig. B).

Fig. B

Shoes 'n' socks

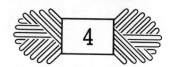

For explanation of project rating, see pg. 3.

The nostalgia craze inspired this design that combines both argyle socks and saddle shoes. These socks are more effective if worn as slippers without shoes; to make them last longer, sew a leather sole to the bottom of each foot. Some knitters may prefer to make only one sock and use it as a unique Christmas stocking to hang on the fireplace. The design is by Nancy Marchant.

You'll need: Fingering yarn — 2 ounces dark green (G), 1 ounce *each* of light yellow (Y), royal blue (B), red (R), white (W), brown (BR), and black (BK); sizes 1 and 3 double-pointed needles; tapestry needle; stitch markers.

GAUGE: 7 stitches=1 inch
9 rows=1 inch (on size 3 needles)

SIZE: 10″ foot, 16″ calf length
Adjust sock measurements as needed.

Knit wit
- Slanting squares on diagram, page 68, indicate decreased stitches.
- When changing from one color to another, always twist yarn once to avoid holes, bringing new color from under old color (see page 14).

Step by step

For key to abbreviations, see pg. 7.

TOP RIBBING—Rnd 1: Using size 1 needles, cast on 92 sts in G. **Rows 2–15:** k 2, p 2 for 15 rows. **Row 16:** Change to size 3 needles. Beg with k row, work in stockinette stitch. Wind 2 bobbins of R, 2 of B, 5 of G. **Row 17:** p 11 G, 1 R, 22 G, 1 B, 22 G, 1 R, 22 G, 1 B, 11 G; turn. **Row 18:** k 10 G, 3 B, 20 G, 3 R, 20 G, 3 B, 20 G, 3 R, 10 G.

Using 2 size 3 needles only, follow rows 19–39, pg. 68.

Row 40: k 11 G, 1 R, 10 G, 2 tog, 10 G, 1 B, 10 G, 2 tog, 10 G, 1 R, 10 G, 2 tog, 10 G, 1 B, 9 G, 2 tog (88 sts). **Row 41:** p 9 G, 3 B, 19 G, 3 R, 19 G, 3 R, 10 G. **Row 42:** k 9 G, 5 R, 17 G, 5 B, 17 G, 5 R, 17 G, 5 B, 8 G. **Row 43:** p 7 G, 7 B, 15 G, 7 R, 15 G, 7 B, 15 G, 7 R, 8 G. **Row 44:** k 2 G tog, k 5 G, 9 R, 6 G, 2 tog, 5 G, 9 B, 6 G, 2 tog, 5 G, 9 R, 6 G, 2 tog, 5 G, 9 B, 6 G (84 sts). **Rows 45–60:** Continue patt in fig. A, pg. 68. **Row 61:** p 10 G, 1 R, 9 G, 2 tog, 9 G, 1 B, 9 G, 2 tog, 9 G, 1 R, 9 G, 2 tog, 9 G, 1 B, 8 G, 2 tog (80 sts). **Row 62:** k 8 G, 3 B, 17 G, 3 R, 17 G, 3 B, 17 G, 3 R, 9 G. **Row 63:** p 8 G, 5 R, 15 G, 5 B, 15 G, 5 R, 15 G, 5 B, 7 G. **Row 64:** k 6 G, 7 B, 13 G, 7 R, 13 G, 7 B, 13 G, 7 R, 7 G. **Row 65:** p 2 tog, 4 G, 9 R, 5 G, 2 tog, 4 G, 9 B, 5 G, 2 tog, 4 G, 9 R, 5 G, 2 tog, 4 G, 9 B, 5 G (76 sts). **Rows 66–79:** Continue patt in fig. A, pg. 68. **Row 80:** k 9 G, 1 R, 8 G, 2 tog, 8 G, 1 B, 8 G, 2 tog, 8 G, 1 R, 8 G, 2 tog, 8 G, 1 B, 7 G, 2 tog (72 sts). **Row 81:** p 7 G, 3 B, 15 G, 3 R, 15 G, 3 B, 15 G, 3 R, 8 G. **Row 82:** k 7 G, 5 R, 13 G, 5 B, 13 G, 5 R, 13 G, 5 B, 6 G. **Row 83:** p 5 G, 7 B, 11 G, 7 R, 11 G, 7 B, 11 G, 7 R, 6 B. **Row 84:** k 2 G tog, 3 G, 9 R, 4 G, 2 tog, 3 G, 9 B, 4 G, 2 tog, 3 G, 9 R, 4 G, 2 tog, 3 G, 9 B, 4 G (68 sts). **Rows 85–96:** Continue patt in fig. A, pg. 68. **Row 97:** Divide sts onto 3 needles. K in the round 17 rnds (23, 22, 23 sts per needle).

HEEL—Place 1ST 17 sts from 1ST needle and 16 sts from 3RD needle on 1 needle. Place rem sts on 2 needles. Work 33 sts on 1ST needle as follows: **Row 1:** Pick up G and k to end of last 17 sts; turn. **Row 2:** p 14 W, 5 BK, 14 W; turn and follow fig. B.

TURN HEEL—Working all sts BR, and turning at end of all rows, continue as follows: **Row 1:** k 19, sl 1, k 1, psso, k 1. **Row 2:** sl 1, p 6, p 2 tog, p 1. **Row 3:** sl 1, k 7, sl 1, k 1, psso, k 1. **Row 4:** sl 1, p 8, p 2 tog, p 1. **Row 5:** sl 1, k 9, sl 1, k 1, psso, k 1. **Row 6:** sl 1, p 10, p 2 tog, p 1. **Row 7:** sl 1, k 11, sl 1, k 1, psso, k 1. **Row 8:** sl 1, p 12, p 2 tog, p 1. **Row 9:** sl 1, k 13, sl 1, k 1, psso, k 1. **Row 10:** sl 1, p 14, p 2 tog, p 1. **Row 11:** sl 1, k 15, sl 1, k 1, psso, k 1. **Row 12:** sl 1, p 16, p 2 tog, p 1. **Row 13:** sl 1, k 17, sl 1, k 1, psso. **Row 14:** p 20 sts. Do not turn.

With right side of work facing you, k across BR, pick up and k 4 more BR and 12 W (these sts go on 1ST needle); place 35 G sts on 2ND needle and k across with G; for 3RD needle, pick up and k 12 W, 4 BR, and 10 BR from 1ST needle. Turn and p 14 BR, 12 W, 35 G, 12 W and 14 BR.

INSTEP—**Row 1:** k 14 BR, 9 W, 2 tog, 2 W, 33 G, 2 W, sl 1, k 1, psso, k 9 W, 14 BR. **Rows 2, 4, 6, 8, and 10:** p in same colors without decreasing. **Row 3:** k 14 BR, 8 W, 2 tog, 3 W, 31 G, 3 W, sl 1, k 1, psso, 8 W, 14 BR. **Row 5:** k 14 BR, 7 W, 2 tog, 4 W, 29 G, 4 W, sl 1, k 1, psso, 7 W, 14 BR. **Row 7:** k 14 BR, 6 W, 2 tog, 5 W, 27 G, 5 W, sl 1, k 1, psso, 6 W, 14 BR. **Row 9:** k 14 BR, 5 W, 2 tog, 6 W, 25 G, 6 W, sl 1, k 1, psso, 5 W, 14 BR. **Row 11:** k 14 BR, 4 W, 2 tog, 7 W,

(Continued on page 69)

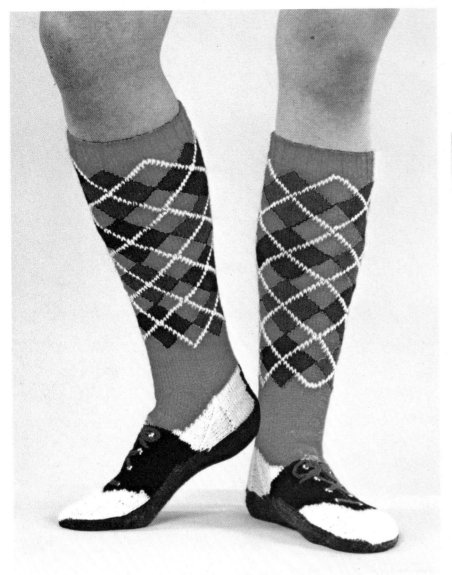

Argyle stripe in duplicate stitch

Turning of heel

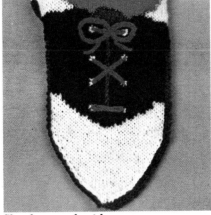

Shoelace embroidery

Royal blue   Dark green   Red

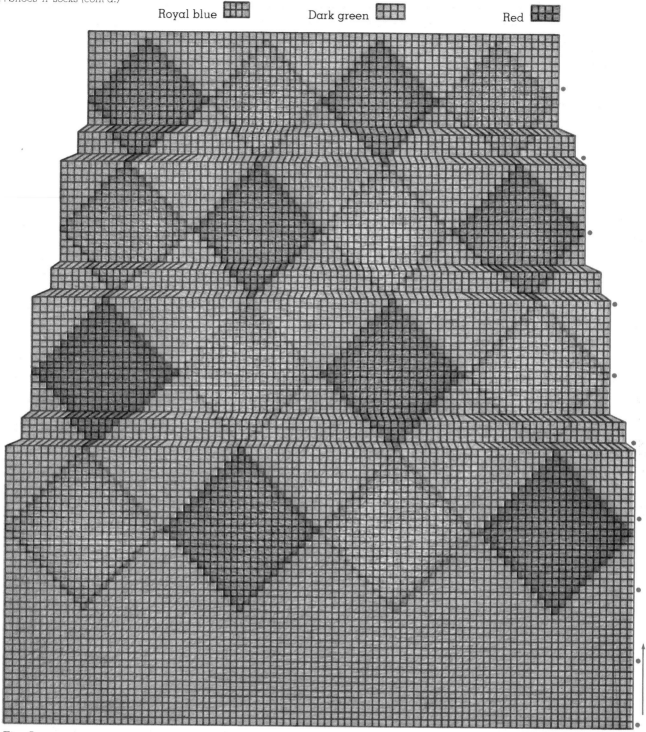

Fig. A

Arrows indicate direction for reading chart.
Dots are placed at 10-row intervals.

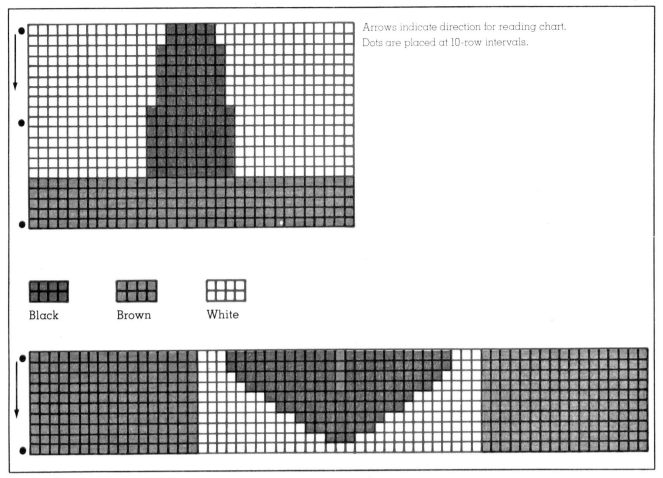

Arrows indicate direction for reading chart.
Dots are placed at 10-row intervals.

Black   Brown   White

23 G, 7 W, sl 1, k 1, psso, 4 W, 14 BR. **Row 12:** p 15 BR, 12 W, 21 G, 12 W, 15 BR. **Row 13:** k 15 BR, 2 W, 2 tog, 9 W, 19 G, 9 W, sl 1, k 1, psso, 2 W, 15 BR. **Row 14:** p 15 BR, 13 W, 17 G, 13 W, 15 BR. **Row 15:** k 15 BR, 1 W, 2 tog, 10 W, 6 G, 5 BR, 6 G, 10 W, sl 1, k 1, psso, 1 W, 15 BR. **Row 16:** p 16 BR, 9 W, 5 BK, 2 G, 7 BR, 2 G, 5 BK, 9 W, 16 BR. **Row 17:** k 15 BR, 2 tog, 3 W, 11 BK, 9 BR, 11 BK, 3 W, sl 1, k 1, psso, k 15 BR. **Row 18:** p 16 BR, 17 BK, 3 BR, 17 BK, 16 BR. **Row 19:** k 14 BR, 2 tog, 18 BK, 1 BR, 18 BK, sl 1, k 1, psso, 14 BR. **Row 20:** p 16 BR, 17 BK, 1 BR, 17 BK, 16 BR. **Row 21:**

k 13 BR, 2 tog, 2 BR, 16 BK, 1 BR, 16 BK, 2 BR, sl 1, k 1, psso, 13 BR. **Row 22:** p 16 BR, 16 BK, 1 BR, 16 BK, 16 BR. **Row 23:** k 12 BR, 2 tog, 3 BR, 15 BK, 1 BR, 15 BK, 3 BR, sl 1, k 1, psso, 12 BR. **Row 24:** p 16 BR, 15 BK, 1 BR, 15 BK, 16 BR. **Row 25:** k 17 BR, 14 BK, 1 BR, 14 BK, 17 BR. **Row 26:** p 17 BR, 14 BK, 1 BR, 14 BK, 17 BR. Rep rows 23 and 24 seven more times, following patt in fig. C. **Row 37:** k 17 BR, 29 W, 17 BR. **Row 38:** p 17 BR, 29 W, 17 BR. **Row 39:** Rep row 37. **Row 40:** p 16 BR, place marker, 1 BR, 29 W, 1 BR, place marker, 16 BR. **Row 41:** k 13 BR, 2 tog, 1 BR, pass marker, 1 BR, sl 1 W, k 1, psso, 25 W, 2 tog, 1 BR, pass marker, 1 BR, sl 1, k 1, psso, 13 BR. **Row 42:** p 16 BR, 27 W, 16 BR. **Row 43:** k 12 BR, 2 tog, 1 BR, pass marker, 1 BR, sl 1 W, k 1, psso, 23 W, 2 tog, 1 BR, pass marker, 1 BR, sl 1, k 1, psso,

12 BR. **Row 44:** p 15 BR, 25 W, 15 BR. **Row 45:** (continuing in BK and W): k to within 3 sts of marker, k 2 tog, k 1, pass marker, k 1, sl 1, k 1, psso, k to within 3 sts of marker, k 2 tog, k 1, pass marker, k 1, sl 1, k 1, psso, k to end. **Row 46:** p.

Rep rows 45 and 46 until 31 sts rem. Then dec in both k and p rows until 11 sts rem, ending with purled row.

FINISHING—Bind off with BR. Leave long tail to sew toe and sock bottom. Using matching yarn and tapestry needle, back stitch (see pg. 16) all seams. Follow photos on pg. 67 to embroider finishing details.

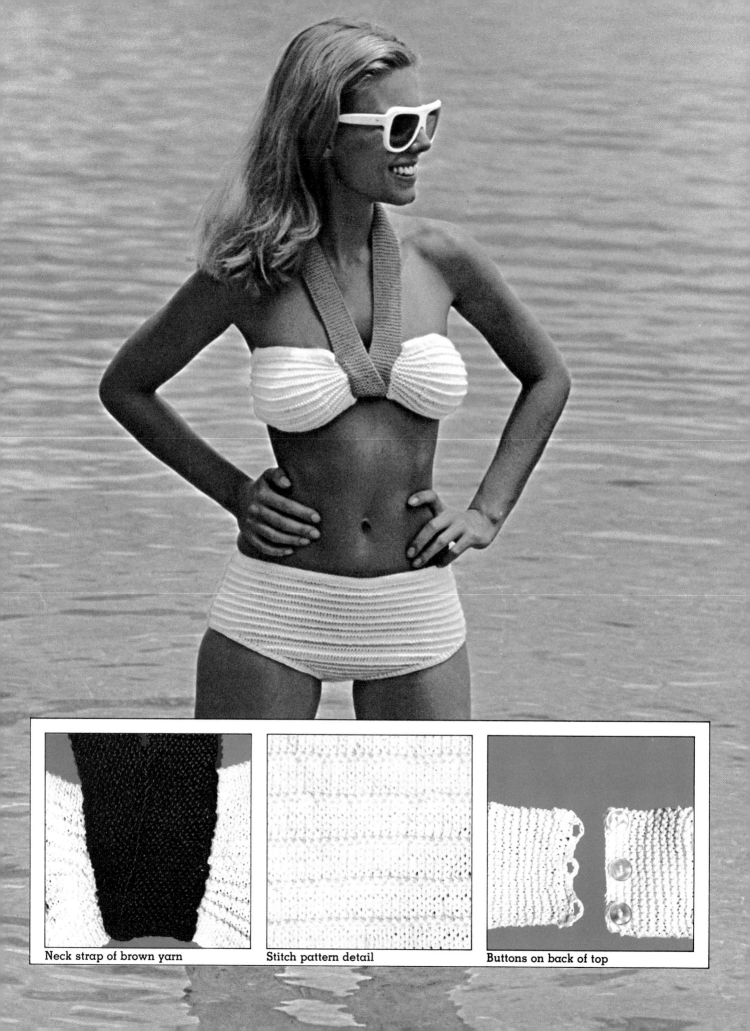

Neck strap of brown yarn

Stitch pattern detail

Buttons on back of top

Bathing suit

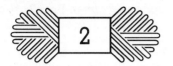

2

For explanation of project rating, see pg. 3.

Designed in France, this knitted two-piece bathing suit can be worn on beaches from Southern France to Southern California. The suit bottom keeps its shape with elastic around the leg openings. The top of the suit has a band that loops around your neck and fastens with three buttons at the back. The design is by *Mon Tricot*.

You'll need: Cotton fingering yarn—6 ounces white (W), 1 ounce green (G); sizes 1 and 2 straight needles; size 4 steel crochet hook; tapestry needle; three ½" buttons; 4½' of ¼"-wide elastic; 6" of ½"-wide white grosgrain ribbon and 8" of 1½"-wide green grosgrain ribbon; sewing needle; white polyester thread; 1 spool white elastic thread; cotton bathing suit liner (optional).

GAUGE: 15 stitches = 2 inches
12 rows = 1 inch (in pattern on size 2 needles)

SIZE: Bust = 32" (34", 36"), hips = 34" (36", 38")
Instructions are for 32" bust and 34" hips; changes for other sizes are in parentheses.

Knit wit

- See information on knitting short rows in **Knit wit** on page 64.

Step by step

For key to abbreviations, see pg. 7.

PANTS—(Beg at top of back.) Using size 2 needles and W, cast on 93 (97, 101) sts. K 1 row, p 1 row for 5 rows, k next row on p side. Rep these 6 rows for patt throughout. Continue in patt, increasing 1 st at each edge of next and every following 3RD row until there are 129 (133, 137) sts. Continue in patt until back measures 5 (5½, 6)".

Begin crotch shaping: Bind off 1 st at beg next 2 rows; bind off 2 sts beg next 4 rows. Rep last 6 rows 9 times more—29 (33, 37) sts rem. Bind off 1 st beg next 10 (14, 18) rows. Bind off 2 sts beg next 2 rows—15 sts rem. Work 20 rows in patt on these sts.

Cast on 1 st beg next 16 (20, 24) rows. Cast on 2 sts beg next 16 rows. Cast on 3 sts beg next 10 rows. Cast on 4 sts beg next 2 rows. Cast on 6 sts beg next 2 rows. Cast on 8 sts beg next 2 rows—129 (133, 137) sts. *Dec 1 st each end of next and every following 3RD row until 93 (97, 101) sts rem. Continue in patt until work measures 5 (5½, 6)" from *. Bind off.

Begin leg bands: (Make 2.) Using size 1 needles and W, pick up and k 158 (164,170) sts evenly around leg edge. Work 3 rows in k 1, p 1 ribbing. Bind off in ribbing.

TOP—(right side) Using size 2 needles and W, cast on 66 (70, 74) sts. Work 12 rows in patt as for pants. K next row. P next row. K 46 (50, 54) sts, turn. In the next row, p 36 (40, 44) sts, turn. K 2 rows on all sts. Rep last 6 rows 8 times more. Work 11 rows in patt over all sts. Bind off. Work left side same as right.

BACK OF TOP—Turn 1ST patt to inside at top and bottom. Whip st in place. With right side facing you, and size 2 needles pick up and k 19 sts along center back edge.

Work 1¾" in garter stitch (see pg. 10). Bind off. Work 2ND side in same manner.

STRAP—Using size 2 needles and G, cast on 12 sts. Work 23 (24, 24)" in garter stitch. Bind off.

FINISHING—Pants: With tapestry needle or crochet hook, join side seams (see pg. 16). Turn 1ST patt to inside at top and whip st loosely in place. Cut elastic to measure and thread through hem. Fasten securely.

Legbands: Using size 1 needles and W, pick up and k 158 (164, 170) sts around leg edge. Work 3 rows in k 1, p 1 ribbing. Bind off in ribbing. Work 2ND band in same manner. Thread tapestry needle with doubled elastic thread and weave in and out of k ribbing sts on wrong side, adjusting to desired fit. Fasten securely.

Top: Thread bottom hems with elastic to measure as in top of pants. With sewing needle and thread, sew strap in position between sides of top and reinforce with 1½" green ribbon. With right side facing you, join yarn to bottom left center edge. Using crochet hook, work buttonholes: *ch 5, skip 3 sts, 4 sc, skip 3 sts, rep from * once, end ch 5, sl st to top edge. Fasten off. Reinforce inside of right center edge with ½" white ribbon and sew buttons opposite buttonholes.

Pullover & socks

See color photo, page 76.

Bicycling, ski touring, and mountaineering are some of the activities that might interest the person who wears our matching sweater and socks. The European-designed socks and sweater use three stitch patterns — diamond, olive and bobble, and cable. The design is by *Mon Tricot*.

You'll need: Knitting worsted — 32 (36) ounces heather blue; sizes 5 and 7 straight needles; size five 16″ circular needle; size 7 double-pointed needles; cable needle; tapestry needle; stitch holder; stitch markers (optional).

GAUGE: 5 stitches=1 inch 7 rows=1 inch (in stockinette stitch on size 7 needles)

SIZE: Chest=40″ (42″) Instructions are for size 40; changes for other size are in parentheses.

Step by step

For key to abbreviations, see pg. 7.

BACK — Using size 5 straight needles, cast on 100 (104) sts and work in k 2, p 2 ribbing for 3″, increasing 1 st beg and end of last row (102, 106 sts). Change to size 7 straight needles.

The following stitch patterns are used in back and throughout project:

Cables (worked on 16 sts): **Row 1:** k 1, *p 2, k 2, rep from * twice more, p 2, k 1. **Rows 2–8:** k the k stitches and p the p stitches. **Row 9:** Sl 4 sts to cable needle and leave at back of work, k 1, p 2, k 1, then (k 1, p 2, k 1) sts from cable needle; sl 4 sts to cable needle and leave at front of work, k 1, p 2, k 1, then (k 1, p 2, k 1) sts from cable needle. **Row 10:** Rep row 2. Rep these 10 rows for cable patt.

Olive and Bobble (worked on 1 st): **Row 1:** In same st, k 1, p 1, k 1, p 1, k 1. **Rows 2, 4, 6, and 8:** p. **Rows 3, 5, 7, and 9:** k. **Row 10:** p 5, yo, pass the 5 purled sts over yo. **Rows 11–14:** Work even in reverse stockinette stitch (see pg. 10). **Row 15:** *Insert right needle as if to k, draw a loop, sl onto left needle and k in loop. Rep from * twice, always inserting needle in same st (3 sts on right needle), then drop initial st from left needle. **Row 16:** p 3, yo, pass the 3 purled sts over yo. **Rows 17–20:** Work even in reverse stockinette stitch. Rep these 20 rows for olive and bobble patt.

Diamonds (worked on 36 sts): **Row 1:** k 1, *p 10, sl 1 st to cable needle and leave at front of work, k next st, then k st from cable needle, rep from * once, p 10, k 1. **Row 2 and all even rows:** k the k sts and p the p sts. **Row 3:** *Cross 2 L (sl 1 st to cable needle and leave at front of work, p 1, k st from cable needle), p 8, cross 2 R (sk first st, k next st, p skipped st, drop both sts off left needle),

rep from * twice. **Row 5:** *p 1, cross 2 L, p 6, cross 2 R, p 1, rep from * twice. **Row 7:** *p 2, cross 2 L, p 4, cross 2 R, p 2, rep from * twice. Continue in this manner, moving k sts every other row until next to each other, then cross sts as in row 1. Move crossed sts away from each other until they meet next k st, then rep row 1. Rep these rows for diamond patt.

Row 1: Work 11 (13) sts reverse stockinette stitch, work 16 sts in cable patt, work 48 sts reverse stockinette stitch, work 16 sts in cable patt, work 11 (13) sts reverse stockinette. **Row 2:** k the k sts and p the p sts. **Row 3:** Continuing reverse stockinette and cables at sides, begin motifs on center 48 sts as follows: Work 3 sts reverse stockinette, olive and bobble patt on next st, 2 sts reverse stockinette, work 36 sts diamond patt, 2 sts reverse stockinette, 1 st olive and bobble patt, 3 sts reverse stockinette. Work even in patt as established until back measures 18 (18½)″ or desired length to underarm.

Diamond stitch pattern

Cable stitch pattern

Shape armholes: Bind off 3 sts beg next 2 rows, then 2 sts beg next 2 rows. Dec 1 st each side every other row 4 times. Work even on rem 84 (88) sts until armholes measure 7½ (8)".

Shape shoulders: At armhole edges, every other row bind off 8 (9) sts twice and 9 sts once. Sl rem 34 sts to holder for back neck.

FRONT—Work same as back until armholes measure 6 (6½)".

Shape neck: Work 31 (33) sts, sl center 22 sts to holder; join 2ND ball to next st and work rem 31 (33) sts. Working both sides at the same time, at neck edges every other row bind off 3 sts, then 2 sts, then 1. Work even on 25 (27) sts until armholes measure same as back. Shape shoulders same as back.

SLEEVES — (Make 2.) Using size 5 straight needles, cast on 44 (48) sts and work in k 2, p 2 ribbing for 3½".

Change to size 7 straight needles and work as follows:
Row 1: 14 (16) sts reverse stockinette, work 16 sts in cable patt, 14 (16) sts reverse stockinette.
Row 2: k the k sts and p the p sts. **Row 3:** Work 10 (12) sts reverse stockinette, work olive and bobble patt on next st, 3 sts reverse stockinette, 16 sts cable, 3 sts reverse stockinette, 1 st olive and bobble patt, 10 (12) sts reverse stockinette.

Continue in patt as established, increasing 1 st each side every 8 rows 10 times. Work evenly on 64 (68) sts until sleeve measures 17¾ (18)" or desired length from beg.

(Continued on next page)

Shape cap: Bind off 3 sts beg next 2 rows and 2 sts beg next 2 rows. Dec 1 st each side every other row 17 (19) times. Work even in patt on rem 20 sts for 5¼ (5½)" for saddle yoke. Bind off.

FINISHING—Join side seams. Join sleeve seams and set in sleeves, placing saddle yoke between front and back. With circular needle, pick up and k 116 (120) sts around neck edge, including sts on holders. Work in k 2, p 2 ribbing for 1¼". Bind off in ribbing. Steam-press seams.

SOCKS—(Make 2.) Using size 5 circular needles, cast on 48 (52) sts, evenly divided. Sl marker on needle to indicate beg of rnds. Work in k 2, p 2 ribbing for 3". Change to size 7 double-pointed needles and begin patt. Work 4 rnds reverse stockinette. **Rnd 5:** Work 20 (24) sts reverse stockinette for back of sock, then work 1 st in olive and bobble patt, 1 st reverse stockinette, 24 sts in diamond patt, 1 st reverse stockinette, 1 st in olive and bobble patt. **Rnds 6–24:** Work even in patt as established. **Rnd 25:** On

center 5 sts at back of leg, dec as follows: p 2 tog, p 1, p 2 tog. Rep dec every 10TH row 3 more times. Continue in patt as established on rem 40 (44) sts until 3 diamonds are completed at center of diamond patt.

Shape heel: Leave 20 (22) front sts on 2 needles for instep and work rem 20 (22) sts in stockinette stitch (see pg. 10) for 2½ (2¾)", ending with purled row. Then, k 11 (12), k 2 tog, turn; sl 1 st, p 2, p 2 tog, turn; sl 1 st, k 3, k 2 tog, turn; sl 1 st, p 4, p 2 tog, turn. Continue in this manner until all sts are worked on both sides, ending with purled row (12 sts rem). K 12 sts, pick up and k 9 (11) sts along left side of heel, p the 20 (22) sts left on needles for instep, pick up and k 9 (11) sts along right side of heel. Keeping front 20 (22) sts in reverse stockinette and 30 sole sts in stockinette, dec as follows: k 2 tog, p 20 (22) front sts, sl 1, k 1, psso, k 26 (30) sts. Rep dec in same place every other rnd 5 more times (38, 44 sts rem). When foot measures 3½ (4)" from heel, continue in stockinette stitch on all sts until foot measures 2" less than desired length.

Shape toe: Dec as follows: k 9 (12), k 2 tog, k 6, sl 1, k 1, psso, k 9, k 2 tog, k 6, sl 1, k 1, psso. Continue to dec in this manner every other rnd on the 6 sts at each side of foot 7 (8) times more (6, 8 sts rem). Join tog by weaving the 3 (4) sts of top of foot with the 3 (4) sts of bottom of foot.

Knit wit
- Stitch markers used between patterns will help you keep track of their progression.
- The less experienced knitter should write out row-by-row instructions until familiar with the patterns.

Olive and bobble stitch pattern

Stitch pattern detail

Flower embroidery detail

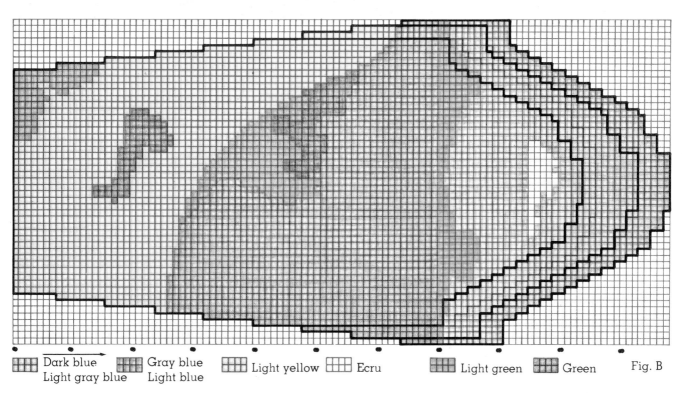

| 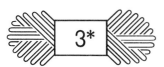 Dark blue | Gray blue | Light yellow | Ecru | Light green | Green | Fig. B |
| Light gray blue | Light blue | | | | | |

Scenic sweater

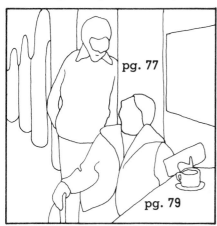

3*

For explanation of project rating, see pg. 3.

Centuries ago, North and Middle American Indians used vividly colored yarns to create "paintings" of ritualistic significance. Today's knitter can use colorful yarns to decorate any garment with landscapes, portraits, or abstract designs. This crew neck sweater pattern recreates a sunny Western landscape complete with green trees, billowy clouds, and blue sky. The design is by Dione King.

pg. 77

pg. 79

You'll need: Knitting worsted — 6 ounces light yellow, 4 ounces *each* of dark blue, light blue, gray blue, light gray blue, gold, and green; 2 ounces dark green; 1 ounce *each* of ecru, golden brown, rust, and cardinal red; sizes 8 and 11 straight needles; size eight 16" circular needle; 2 stitch holders, tapestry needle; stitch markers; yarn bobbins.

GAUGE: 3 stitches= 1 inch
5 rows= 1 inch

SIZE: Chest = 36" (42", 44")
Instructions are for size 36; changes for other sizes are in parentheses.

Knit wit

- Stockinette stitch (see page 10) used throughout unless otherwise indicated.
- Use two strands knitting worsted throughout. Colors are indicated together (see figures A and B).
- Wind bobbins with combined strands before beginning project.
- For a better pattern match down side seams, reverse chart for back.

Step by step

For key to abbreviations, see pg. 7.

BACK —Using size 8 straight needles and gold, cast on 54 (62, 66) sts. Work in k 1, p 1 ribbing for 10 rows, increasing 1 st at end of 10TH row. Change to size 11 straight needles; work 64 (64,66) rows, following fig. A, pg. 78.

Armholes: Bind off 4 sts at beg of next 2 rows. Dec 1 st each end every other row twice. Work even on 43 (51, 55) sts for 32 (36, 38) rows.

Shoulders: Bind off 6 (8, 9) sts at beg of next 2 rows and 7 (8, 9) sts in next 2 rows. Sl rem 17 (19, 19) sts on stitch holder.

FRONT —Work same as back, following fig. A for 18 (20, 22) rows above 1ST armhole bind-off, ending with purled row.

Neck: Work 17 (21, 23) sts. Sl center 9 sts on stitch holder. Join another 2-strand ball of yarn to next st; work across. Working both sides at once, dec 1 st at neck edge every other row 4 (5, 5) times. Work even until front measures same as back.

(Continued on next page)

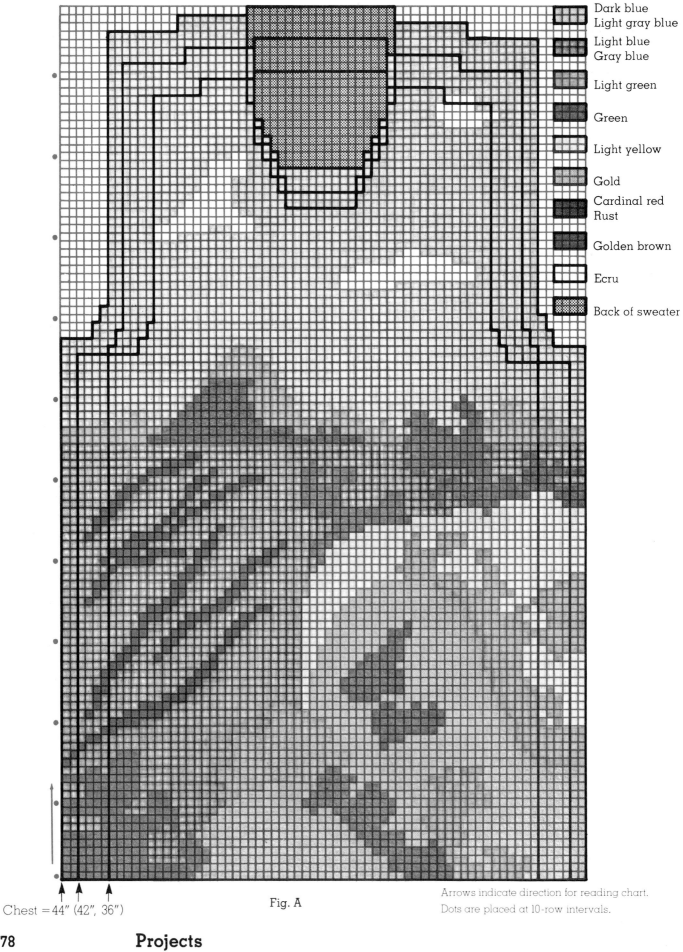

Dark blue
Light gray blue

Light blue
Gray blue

Light green

Green

Light yellow

Gold

Cardinal red
Rust

Golden brown

Ecru

Back of sweater

Fig. A

Chest = 44" (42", 36")

Arrows indicate direction for reading chart.

Dots are placed at 10-row intervals.

Shoulders: Bind off 6 (8, 9) sts at beg of next 2 rows and 7 (8, 9) sts in next 2 rows.

SLEEVES — (Make 2.) Beg at lower edge. Using size 8 straight needles and light yellow, cast on 34 sts. Work in k 1, p 1 ribbing for 10 rows, increasing 1 st at end of 10TH row. Change to size 11 straight needles. Follow fig. B, increasing 1 st each side every 8TH row 5 (7, 8) times. Continue in patt on 45 (49, 51) sts for 70 (76, 80) rows from beg of stockinette stitch.

Sleeve cap: Bind off 4 sts at beg of next 2 rows. Dec 1 st each side every other row 9 (10, 11) times. Bind off 3 sts at beg of next 4 rows. Bind off rem 7 (9, 9) sts.

FINISHING — Using double strand of gray blue and light gray blue, join shoulder seams. Join double strand of gray blue and light gray blue to first st on back neck stitch holder. Using circular needle, k off 17 (19, 19) sts from holder; pick up and k 16 (18, 20) sts to front holder; k off 9 sts from holder; pick up and k 16 (18, 20) sts to shoulder seam. Sl marker on needle. Work in k 1, p 1 ribbing for 5 rnds. Bind off loosely with size 11 straight needles in ribbing.

With double strand of light yellow, join side seams and sleeve seams. Set in sleeves.

Alpine sweater

See color photo, page 76.

For explanation of project rating, see pg. 3.

Embroidered, cabled sweaters have long been the traditional style in Alpine villages. The design is by *Mon Tricot.*

You'll need: Knitting worsted — 36 (40, 40) ounces ecru; sizes 7, 8, and 10 straight needles; cable needle; 3 stitch holders; tapestry needle; 9' of scrap yarn in red, blue, green, and yellow for embroidery; five ⅞" buttons.

GAUGE: 4 stitches= 1 inch (reverse stockinette stitch on size 10 needles)

SIZE: Bust =34" (36", 38") Instructions are for size 34; changes for other sizes are in parentheses.

Knit wit
- Entire sweater knitted with double strand of yarn.

Step by step

For key to abbreviations, see pg. 7.

BACK — Using size 8 needles, cast on 60 (64, 68) sts. Work in k 1, p 1 ribbing for 3", increasing 16 sts evenly spaced across last row (76, 80, 84) sts.

Stitch patts: (twist stitches and diamonds) Twist stitches = 4 sts. **Row 1:** *k in back loop of 2ND st, then k first st, dropping both sts from left needle. Rep from * once. **Row 2:** *Skip first st, p in front of 2ND st, p skipped st, dropping both off left needle. Rep from * once. Rep these 2 rows for twist stitches.

Diamonds: (14 sts) — **Row 1:** p 5, k 4, p 5. **Row 2 and all even rows:** k the k sts and p the p sts. **Row 3:** p 5, sl 2 sts onto cable needle and leave at front of work, k 2, k sts from cable needle, p 5. **Row 5:** p 4, cross 3 R (sl 1 st to cable needle and leave at back of work, k 2, p cable st), cross 3 L (sl 2 sts to cable needle and leave at front of work, p 1, k 2 cable sts), p 4. **Row 7:** p 3, cross 3 R, p 2, cross 3 L, p 3. **Row 9:** p 2, cross 3 R, p 4, cross 3 L, p 2. **Row 11:** p 1, cross 3 R, p 6, cross 3 L, p 1. **Row 13:** Cross 3 R, p 8, cross 3 L. **Row 15:** Cross 3 L, p 8, cross 3 R. **Row 17:** p 1, cross 3 L, p 6, cross 3 R, p 1. Continue moving the k sts toward center until 4 sts in center. **Rows 25 and 29:** Same as row 3. **Row 27:** Same as row 1. **Row 30:** Same as row 2. Rep these 30 rows for patt.

Change to size 10 needles and work as follows: 5 (6, 7) sts reverse stockinette stitch, cable 4, p 3, 14 sts in diamond patt, p 3, cable 4, 10 (12, 14) sts in reverse stockinette stitch, cable 4, p 3, 14 sts diamond patt, p 3, cable 4, 5 (6, 7) sts reverse stockinette. Work in patt as established until back measures 14½ (15, 15½)" or desired length to underarm.

Shape armholes: Continuing patt, bind off 4 (5, 6) sts beg next 2 rows. Work even on rem 68 (70, 72) sts until armholes measure 7 (7½, 8)" above bind-off or desired length, ending with wrong side row worked.

Shape shoulders: Bind off 8 sts beg next 4 rows and 7 sts beg next 2 rows. Sl rem 22 (24, 26) sts to stitch holder.

LEFT FRONT — Using size 8 needles, cast on 30 (32, 34) sts. Work in k 1, p 1 ribbing for 3", increasing 6 sts evenly spaced across last row.

Change to size 10 needles and work 36 (38, 40) sts as follows: 5 (6, 7) sts reverse stockinette stitch, cable 4, p 3, 14 sts diamond patt, p 3, cable 4, 3 (4, 5) sts reverse stockinette. Work in patt as established until front measures same as

(Continued on next page)

back to underarm, ending
with wrong side row worked.

Shape armhole: Bind off 4 (5, 6)
sts beg next row. Work even on
rem 32 (33, 34) sts until armhole
measures 5 (5½, 6)" above
bind-off, ending with right
side row worked.

Shape neck: Bind off 5 (5, 6) sts
beg next row. Dec 1 st at neck
edge every row 4 (5, 5) times.
When armhole measures same
as back, bind off for shoulder.
From armhole edge, bind off
8 sts twice, 7 sts once.

RIGHT FRONT—Work same as
left front, reversing all shaping.

SLEEVES—(Make 2.) Using size
8 needles, cast on 36 (38, 40)
sts. Work in k 1, p 1 ribbing
for 3", increasing 20 sts evenly
spaced across last row.

Change to size 10 needles
and work as follows on 56

(58, 60) sts: 14 (15, 16) sts
reverse stockinette stitch,
cable 4, p 3, 14 sts diamond
patt, p 3, cable 4, 14 (15, 16) sts
reverse stockinette stitch. Work
even in patt as established
until sleeve measures 20½
(21½, 22)" or desired length.
Bind off.

LEFT FRONT BAND—Using
size 8 needles, cast on 9 sts.
Work in garter stitch (see pg.
10) until band is long enough
to reach from bottom of left
front to bound-off sts at neck
edge. Sl sts to holder.

RIGHT FRONT BAND—Cast
on and work same as for left
front for ¾". **Buttonhole row:**
k 3, bind off next 3 sts, k 3. On
next row, cast on 3 sts over
bound-off sts. Count rem
garter stitch ridges, divide by
4, and work 4 more buttonholes evenly spaced, with last

buttonhole 2 ridges below
bound-off sts at neckline. Sl
sts to holder.

FINISHING—Join shoulder,
side and sleeve seams. Set
sleeves into armholes. Join
borders to front edges.

Collar: Using size 7 needles, k off
9 sts from right band. Pick up
and k 5 (5, 6) bound-off neck
sts, *pick up and k 8 (10, 10)
sts along shaped neck edge*.
K off 22 (24, 26) sts from back
neck holder. Rep from * to *
once. Pick up and k 5 (5, 6)
bound-off neck sts, k off 9 sts
from left band. Work in garter
stitch on 64 (72, 76) sts for 6
rows. Change to size 10
needles and continue until
collar measures 5½". Bind off
loosely.

Sew on buttons. Embroider
flowers (see photo detail,
pg. 76).

Index